KINDS OF BELIEVERS

Why All God's Children Are Not Blessed Equally

ABRAHAM JOHN

SEVEN KINDS OF BELIEVERS
Why all God's Children Are Not Blessed Equally

First Edition © 2004 by Abraham John
Second Edition © 2025 by Abraham John

Published by Abraham John
www.TheKingdomNetwork.org
info@thekingdomnetwork.org
1-(800)-558-5020

ISBN: 978-1-948330-31-2

Unless otherwise indicated, Scripture quotations are from the New King James Version of the Bible (Italics added).

Scripture quotations marked (KJV) are from the King James Version of the Bible (Italics added.). Scripture quotations marked (AMB) are from the Amplified Version of the Bible.

Printed and Published in the United States of America.

All rights reserved. No part of this book may be reproduced or translated or transmitted in any form or by any other means, electronic, mechanical, including photocopying, recording, or by any information storage and retrieval system, without permission in writing from the publisher.

I dedicate this book to the Holy Spirit—my Mentor, Teacher, Comforter and Counselor—the Spirit of Truth who teaches me all things.

Table of Contents

Preface	7
Introduction	13
Chapter 1: The Origin of Man	17
Chapter 2: Seven Kinds of Believers	37
First Kind: Saved, but Trapped in Egypt	39
Chapter 3: The Brother of the Prodigal	45
Second Kind: Saved, but Often Takes Trips Back to Egypt	57
Chapter 4: The Blessing of the Prodigal	63
Third Kind: Only Men and Children are Saved	73
Chapter 5: Spiritual Blessings	77
Fourth Kind: Only Wives Are Saved	97
Chapter 6: Understanding Spiritual Warfare	101
Fifth Kind: Saved, but Material Blessings Remain in Egypt	109
Chapter 7: Be Born Again	115
Sixth Kind: Saved but Stuck in the Wilderness	125
Chapter 8: Seeing and Entering the Kingdom of God	131
Seventh Kind: Saved and Inherited the Promised Land	163
Chapter 9: Inheriting the Kingdom of God	167
More Books & Resources	**175**

Preface

Have you ever thought, whether God loves us all the same, then why isn't everyone equally blessed in the church? Everyone who goes to church sings the same songs, partakes of the same communion, hears the same message, and receives the same prayers. We all have the same Father, and read the same Bible; but when it comes to receiving blessings, we still have both rich and poor, sick and healed in the church.

In the Old Testament everyone was equally blessed, and there were no sick or feeble among them. Psalm 105:37 says, "He also brought them out with silver and gold, and there was none feeble among His tribes."

The Bible says that we received a better covenent than they have, and the penalty for sin has been paid in full; death and the grave have no more power over us. We have received a more glorious ministry than they had.

2 Corinthians 3:7 we read, "But if the ministry of death, written and engraved on stones, was glorious, how will the ministry of the spirit not be more glorious?" Old Testament saints looked forward to enjoying and experiencing the day that we are living in.

Unfortunately, some of us still look back, desiring to have what the Old Testament saints had.

Have you ever been jealous of seeing someone get blessed? Let me be honest with you; I have felt those pricks in my heart too, because I don't always have the means to do the ministry that some others have.

The Bible says we are all the children of the same Father. He loves all His children equally. He doesn't show partiality, and He is not a respecter of persons.

After the resurrection, Jesus told His disciples that He is going to His Father and our Father. John 20:17 says, "I am ascending to My Father and your Father, and to my God and your God."

The Bible says if God didn't spare His Son, but delivered Him up for us all, how shall he not with Him also freely give us all things? (Romans 8:32).

The Bible called Adam the son of God (Luke 3:38). When God created Adam, His son, He did everything according to His capacity in order to provide for His son. But because of Adam's and Eve's spiritual deaths, we lost the sonship and every material blessing with it.

We lost the garden, the glory of God, health, wisdom, wealth, the ability to see into and know the spirit world; and so, we became limited, ordinary human beings.

My question is—if we lost all because of sin and being spiritually dead, wouldn't all be restored when we are made spiritually alive?

I believe with all my heart that is what Christ did on the cross for us. I believe that is what "redemption" is all about. He was restoring or redeeming everything we lost and reconciling us to God, making us sons of God again.

That is why we read in John 1:12 that, "But as many as received Him, to them He gave the right to become children of God."

Any time you think about yourself as other than a child of God, that thought is from the flesh or the devil. We must constantly educate our mind to think and act like a son of God.

This is what the Bible calls renewing our mind. Our unrenewed mind is used to thinking rotten, stinky, and negative thoughts, and will always give you an opinion about yourself that is not true. We inherited that from our past generations. From Adam to your father, every little bit of junk from every human who lived before, has been passed down to us.

This book is for those who go to church faithfully and do all they can to achieve their goals, but are still not finding the light at the other end of the tunnel they seek. You may be paying tithes and offerings, reading your Bible every day; but just don't know what is going on. What has gone wrong? Your life keep going around in circles?

Hebrews 9:13, 14 says, "For if the blood of bulls and goats and the ashes of a heifer, sprinkling the unclean, sanctifies for the purifying of the flesh, how much more shall the blood of Christ, who through eternal Spirit offered Himself without spot to God, cleanse your conscience from dead works to serve the living God?"

I was talking to a friend of mine, and what she said, grieved my spirit. She said we cannot have what the Bible says we can have because we are not "there" yet. Some believe we have to wait until we get old in order to receive what the Bible says.

Spiritual maturity doesn't come with age. If it was so, our grandparents would be the most spiritual giants alive on the earth. You don't have to wait to get old to become spiritual. Don't be deceived; the Bible was given to us not to tell us just about life in heaven, but also to enjoy the blessings it promises here on earth.

Why aren't all children of God equally blessed? This has been a genuine question in the minds of many faithful Christians for centuries.

In a miracle crusade, some walk way healed, while others go back to their homes with the same sickness, thinking God doesn't love them as much as He does those who received their healing instantly.

This book cane about as a result of my own seeking the answers to the above questions. Many Christians that I know, struggle financially, not having enough. I struggled in my life for many years, and I still wonder sometimes these days. Nevertheless, by God's grace, I am well on my way to fulfilling the call God has for me.

The Bible says in Psalm 34:10 "The young lions lack and suffer hunger; but those who seek the Lord shall not lack any good thing."

Did you experience any lack in the past month or two?

The Bible says in 1 Peter 2:24 "... By whose stripes you were healed."

Have you lately seen or visited a friend or relative who has been sick?

I believe all the answers to the above questions should be *Yes*.

Have you heard of a business man in your church who just bought a new car for $75,000, and you can't even afford a car? Or, perhaps you know of someone who bought a new six-bedroom house for only them and their spouse to live in it.

What is wrong? Is God partial? Does He have favorites?

You may have been working so hard for a few years to simply save extra money so you can buy a piece of furniture that you like or some clothes from your dream fashion shop. You thought the only way to get the extra money was to work harder or extra hours; only to find that your body is not cooperating with your mind and moves slower than you want. You get bitter at life and yourself.

Dear child of God, don't be disappointed. God loves you the same just as He loves anyone else. Take courage, you too can achieve your goals and dreams. Just like the father of the prodigal son told his elder son. "Son, you are always with me, and all that I have is yours" (Luke 15:31).

All that God has is yours because you are His child. If we are God's children, then we are co-heirs with Christ (Romans 8:16, 17). God has made all He has available for our disposal. We simply just don't know yet how to receive it.

Well, I believe that is precisely why God has made me write this wonderful book, with folk like you in mind.

The spirit of the Lord revealed to me that there are seven kinds of believers in the church. Each one receives what God has made available to them according to their faith to receive it.

God has made equal blessings available to all of us. However, He will not force His blessings upon you or anyone. It is up to us to find them out, and then to possess them, just like the Israelites did in their Promised Land.

Just because God had given them the promise, they didn't automatically inherit the land. They had to fight and dispossess their enemies before they could have the land. As someone said, "If it is up to me, then it is up to me."

We are going to explore the Holy Scriptures to see how all our needs can be met in Christ Jesus.

Abraham John

Introduction

"In life you don't get what you deserve, but what you fight for." The Holy Spirit has prompted me and given the words for this book, for those dear children of God who have done everything they know how, and still can't move ahead in life.

This book is for those dear believers who are asking themselves the question, "Is this all there is for me, in my Christian life?

You may have started to accept where you are in life, and what you have right now as if *that* is all you're ever going to get from God. It is also for others, too, if you are at the point of compromise because you are tired of fighting and do not want to hold on any longer.

This book is for those who know in their spirit what they can achieve, but somehow their soul and body seem not there yet.

This is based on an account of my personal journey with the Lord. As His Word says, we go from glory to glory. This is what He wants for you too, instead of you having to go from one problem to the other; thinking, is all this ever going to end for me?

It's not unusual for believers go from problem to problem, lurching from one challenge to the next one.

I have no doubt this book will equip you with the revelation you need to go to the next level. This is *revelation* and not information. Information comes from learning and inquiring. Revelation comes when you have an experience with God and His Word. This is what I am inviting you to have out of this book—an experience with God.

You might have all the right information, but without an experience with God, that information is just head knowledge. I haven't done any research of any kind other than the Holy Word of God in order to write this book.

In boxing, whoever throws the last blow, wins. Many have received blows from the enemy and struck down to the ground. God is saying don't stay on the floor. Get up; it is time to fight. As the Bible says in 2 Samuel 10:12, "Be of good courage, and let us be strong for our people and for the cities of our God. And may the LORD do what is good in His sight."

Dear Child of God, let me tell you something that will likely startle you. The world is in chaos, not because of the devil, but because of us! It is because we Christians don't do what we say we should.

The majority, however, don't seem to know how they should live out what the Word says about them.

So, let me tell you about my life:

> I wanted to live the way the Word says I should. I tried it more times than I can count, and I didn't get anywhere in life. I took one step forward and seven backwards. I was trying to reach something which was beyond my apprehension.
>
> I had to *re*-construct and *re*-program my mind, my theology and my heart, before I could take a new step of faith.

One | Introduction

God said to Jeremiah that He had given him power to throw down, to pull down and to root out (Jeremiah 1:10). Jeremiah had to do those three things before he could build and plant.

Many times, we try to build and to plant before we throw down, pull down, and root out the old.

If you are ready for a change and fresh fire from God, please read on.

One thing I can say for sure is, He is not done with you yet. He has much more in store for you than what you have dared to imagine. He has more things for you to do than you ever thought possible. He loves you far more than you can merely think of in your mind.

This book contains revelations from God's Word that changed my life. They helped me to find my way when I reached my dead-end. These served as guide-posts, to lead me to the threshold of next open door. These are supernatural keys that unlock divine wisdom and might as we travel the narrow path of life.

CHAPTER ONE

The Origin of Man

The first step in receiving the blessings of God in our lives is to see how we started out in the beginning. If we know where we come from and what we had in our lives, it is easy to go back and receive it again.

How did God create us? How did He expect us to live? What are the things He gave us when He created us? Which are the things we lost as the result of fall? How do we go back to receive them again? Did God ever change His original purpose and plan about humanity? Why did He create man?

These are some of the questions I would like to answer in this chapter.

When God created the human race there was only one "kind" of believer in the beginning. Adam before the fall is the only prototype we should follow. Our foremost desire should be to become like Adam was before the fall.

Luke chapter 3:38b says, "... Adam was the son of God." Our forefather, Adam, was the son of God just like Jesus is the Son of

God. What does that mean? When God created Adam, he had the same qualities that God has. Those who saw Adam would recognize who his father was.

Just like in the natural realm, when we see somebody, the first thing we want to know is their name and where they are from.

In the phrase, "son of God," if you look at this carefully, we see something powerful. The word "of" is what makes all the difference. If we look into the grammar and study the use of the word "of," it is used to explain possession, and what the relation is to the subject being talked about; so, it refers *to whom* something belongs, in order to tell *where* something came from. When we use "of" it shows to whom we belong, and where we come from.

If we say a candy is made *of* chocolate, that candy is full of chocolate. The kitten of a cat will be a cat, and the calf of an elephant will be an elephant. A cat never gives birth to dogs, and an elephant never gives birth to cats.

We are going to see from the scriptures when God created Adam, the things He gave to His son.

As a parent we do our best to provide for and nurture our children. We buy things according to our capacity and send them to the school that we can afford. When God created His son, Adam, He did everything according to His capacity to provide for his son. Imagine that; God who is unlimited in power, wisdom, love, and wealth did everything for Adam to make his life enjoyable on the earth.

We don't expect our children to get sick and fail in their lives. We don't give them sickness because they didn't do their homework or chores. The Bible says, "If you then, being evil, know how to give good gifts to your children, how much more will your Father who is in heaven give good things to those who ask Him!" (Matthew 7:11).

So far, I have never seen any parents bringing the germs of diseases, to give to their kids to punish them because they love them so much! If they do that, they are insane and have lost their minds. God never expected His Adam to get sick, to become poor, disappointed, and discouraged. We don't expect our children to become poor and destitute and live in a shambles. We expect them to do better than we did and have good things in their lives. We expect and train our children not to make the same mistakes that we made; and it brings joy to our hearts when we see our children excel in things that we couldn't. What a dishonorable thought that would be—to think that our Heavenly Father would expect evil for us, and not the opposite!

Religion has done a 'good' job in many lives causing belief that God is after them to punish them, make them fail, and give sickness to teach them character, or make them more holy. I rebuke that religious spirit and cast it out in Jesus' name. Our God is a good God, and whatever comes from Him is good.

The Bible says "Every good gift and every perfect gift is from above. And comes down from the Father of lights, with whom there is no variation or shadow of turning" (James 1:17). If something is good and perfect, it is from God. If something is bad and ugly, it is from the devil. It is that plain and simple to understand.

So far, I have not seen a sickness that is "good" and poverty that is "perfect." If you believe that God gives sickness, or if someone you know says that it is God's will for him or her to be sick, tell them not to go to the hospital or use any medication. If they do, they are going against the will of God. Just stay home and be happy about your sickness. No, dear child of God, our God is a good God. He cannot produce two different kinds of springs from the same source (James 3:11-12).

You might ask, then why does the Bible say that God chastises whom He loves? (Hebrews 12:5-6).

If you want to know more about chastisement, please read my book, *Overcoming the Spirit of Poverty*, where I covered this topic in detail. We don't spank or chastise our children when they return from the school with a trophy in their hands. We chastise them when they disobey us. We make them sit in the corner, or however you chose to do so.

The Bible says God is love; He is nothing else but love. We don't understand God's love. The Apostle Paul explained it the best he could in first Corinthians chapter thirteen. Please read and compare that with the image which you have of God in your heart. I am sure we all have to make some adjustments about our image of God. I have had to do so, big time.

We are going back to look in the book of Genesis to see how God created us, and what things He has given us as His children. There are eight things that God gave us when He created us in the beginning.

1) Image and Likeness

The first thing God gave us when He created us was His likeness and image. "Then God said, let us make man in our image, according to our likeness ..." Genesis 1:26. We are created in the image and likeness of God.

This doesn't mean we look like God in our physical appearance. In creation God spoke to the materials He created to bring out whatever He intended to create. He spoke to the water to bring forth fishes and all sea creatures and birds of the air. Did you know that birds came out of water? (Genesis 1:20). He spoke to the earth to bring forth animals and creeping creatures, and it was so. When He created man, He spoke to Himself and said "Let Us …" The Bible says in John 4:24, "God is Spirit …"

He created us after his likeness and image, and He is Spirit. He formed our body from the dust. We are not our body; we are a spirit living in a body. So, the image and likeness means that our spirit has the same qualities that God has.

We have His wisdom, His power, His glory, and His holiness, etc.

2) God breathed His Spirit into us

The second thing God did when created us was to breathe His Spirit into our nostrils. Genesis 2:7 says, "And the LORD God formed man of the dust of the ground, and breathed into his nostrils the breath of life; and man became a living being." You may say, "He didn't breathe into my nostrils; it was Adam's nostrils."

Do you believe this? Whatever happened to Adam also happened to you, for he is our prototype. Our body was formed from the dust and didn't have any life until God breathed the breath of life. I can accept what religion says if God has created a living soul from the earth just like He created other creatures, and then breathed His Spirit into us. The Bible says we had no life in us until He breathed the breath of life, His Spirit.

Wow! We have the same Spirit that God has. Do you know what makes a spirit, a *spirit*? A *spirit* means "life," and it is not limited by time and space. A spirit is unlimited; otherwise it is not a spirit, but a material body. This means we have an unlimited spirit living inside of us. We are limited only to our body, but our spirit has unlimited capacity and potential waiting to be released.

If a man decides to go to the moon, he can do it. If he decides to go Mars, he can do it. If he decides to climb Mount Everest or even build a city in outer space, he can do it. God said in Genesis 11:6 (KJV), "And the Lord said, behold, the people is one, and they have all one language; and this they begin to do; and now nothing will be restrained from them, which they have imagined to do."

You better believe what God says about you, and not what your grandpa told you. Only man has the capacity and creativity to imagine and make something like God has made. No animal has that power in them. It is because we have received our spirit from God.

When God breathed His Spirit into us, everything that God has—His wisdom, His love, and His creativity—went into us. That is why Adam could name all the animals and creatures in one day (Genesis 2:19). Imagine the brain power Adam had before the fall!

When man transgressed God's Word, he died as God said that we would, but it was a spiritual death. We lost everything that God had given us, and we inherited a mindset" you and I had until we were "born again." *Born again* means our spirit is being made alive in God a second time. I believe that whatever we lost because of spiritual death, we will receive back when we are spiritually alive again.

God does not have sons *and* daughters. He has only *sons*. Hold on sisters, I will explain it; so please don't throw the book away. When God made Eve from Adam's rib, He did not breathe into her a second time. The same spirit that was in Adam came into Eve. It was the spirit of his son, Adam. The spirit that is in woman and man is the same spirit, and that is the spirit of sonship. The Bible says in Romans 8:15, "For you did not receive the spirit of bondage again to fear, but you received the Spirit of adoption by whom we cry out, "Abba, Father."

This means, when you are born again, whether you are a man or a woman, that same spirit is renewed in you. The function of your body may differ from male and female, but the function of the spirit does not change. Woman is not inferior to man in her spirit; but she has to submit to the man, because she came out of the man; and the spirit she received is of the man.

3) Dominion

The third thing that God gave to us when He created us is dominion. Genesis 1:26 says, "... let them have dominion over the fish of the sea, over the birds of the air, and over the cattle, over all the earth."

What is dominion? Dominion is doing what is right no matter what the cost. Dominion is not so much controlling animals and nature, as we think. Dominion is self-control. Self-control means to be ruled by the spirit, and not by our senses or emotions. We are not controlled by any outside force. Our spirit is in charge of our lives, and when our spirit is in charge of our lives, everything else will fall right into place.

Many are victims of their circumstances. Their circumstances decide their attitudes. One thing that we inherited because of the fall is the tendency to blame something or someone else for our faults.

When you have dominion or self-control, you won't blame anyone for your faults. You will accept responsibility, and try to make things better than they appear. Dominion is more doing what is right rather than not doing what is wrong. We can stop doing what is wrong, but that won't help. We have to do what is right when it seems impossible. This is self-control or dominion, which pushes us to become people of excellence, and the light of this world.

Today, people are happy when they hear about taking dominion. I was preaching one day in a church about dominion, and one man stood up and said, "That means I can control and have authority over my wife." No, that is not what God meant by dominion.

Others run around looking for demons to take dominion of when they can't even control their own lust or passions. Dear saints of God, let us take responsibility for our emotions and actions and become people of self-control; then the world will be attracted to the church.

Dominion or self-control is a fruit of the spirit (Galatians 5:22). The Bible says, "Whoever has no rule over his own spirit is like a city broken down, without walls" (Proverbs 25 :28). I have seen tongue-talking, holy-rolling Christians turning their faces red like a burning sun over situations with a mate or friends. The Bible says, "Do not hasten in your spirit to be angry. For anger rests in the bosom of fools" (Ecclesiastes 6:3).

Let us have control over our own spirit and emotions before we go out to defeat demons and principalities. I have seen people who have great talents and the call of God on them, messing up their own lives for a lack of self-control; then they blame the devil for their foolish actions. I have seen people cry over every situation; when they hear about a squirrel that was run over by a car, they would start crying.

Take dominion, dear child of God, because you have been created in the image and likeness of God. God, who is all-powerful, can do anything He wants to; but He will not because he has dominion and controls Himself or limits Himself to His Word.

When the Roman soldiers came to arrest Jesus, Peter took the sword and cut off one servant's ear. Jesus said, "Or do your think that I cannot now pray to My Father, and He will provide Me with more than twelve legions of angels?" (Matthew 26:53). He did not do that because He had to follow the plan He had received from the Father (Matthew 26:54).

4) Seed

The fourth thing God gave to us when He created us was seed. "And God said, See, I have given you every herb that yields seed which is on the face of all the earth ..." (Genesis 1:29).

Everything God gives to us comes in the form of a seed. The Word of God is a seed, and we have been born again by the incorruptible seed of the Word of God (1 Peter 1:23). The whole earth is functioning under the principle of sowing and reaping.

The Bible says, "... Whatever a man sows, that he will also reap" (Galatians 6:7b). Whatever you have today is the harvest of the seed you have sown yesterday or last year. Your finances reflect the seed you have sown. Your words are seeds, and they will bring forth the harvest for better or for worse. Your life itself is a seed, and God expects a harvest from whatever He has given you.

A seed is something that has the unlimited potential to reproduce its own kind. As we heard before, "You can count the seeds in an apple, but you cannot count the apples in a seed." That is the best way to explain the principle of sowing and reaping.

God has given each of us something, and it is in a seed form. You need to invest it, and then wait for the harvest. The parable of the talents is the best way to see what God expects from each of us. He expects us to multiply our seeds, and then we will be called good and faithful servants.

Whatever you have today has got unlimited potential to reproduce its own kind.

Some of you have heard me tell this story:

> I started this ministry in 1995, sowing by faith in order to support a missionary with twenty-five cents per month. I

was a part of a team that did door-to-door evangelism in the northern part of India.

My team leader was a convert from Hinduism, and his name was Ibo. He was the only person who became a Christian from his family. So, his family and community ostracized him, and he didn't have any financial support. We did evangelism for three months, and the time came for us to go back to our base.

The day we departed, Ibo came and asked if I would support him with 25 cents (10 Rupees in Indian currency) per month. I didn't know what to reply to him, because I didn't have 25 cents; and if I said yes, I didn't know where I would get that money from.

I thought for a minute, and the Holy Spirit gave me the faith to tell him that I was going to support him with 25 cents per month. One month passed since we departed; God gave me 25 cents, and I sent him that amount of money. What if I would have eaten that seed and not kept my commitment? I would still be in the same place financially that I was ten years ago.

Thank God for the grace to obey His voice! The next month God gave me 50 cents, and I sent that money to Ibo. On the third month, God gave 75 cents, and it grew every month until it grew up to 45 dollars per month. God blessed Ibo and opened a door for him to take higher education. Today he is doing his PhD in theology in the USA, and he is the first one from his community to study at that level. He and his wife are in charge of our second orphanage in Manipur.

The twenty-five cents that I sowed by faith, even though I didn't have it in my hand, reproduced a harvest that even amazes me today. You can only expect from something what you are willing to let go of from your hand.

Today, when I look back, we have helped establish 70 churches, conducted 30 crusades, established three orphanages, supported 50 pastors and their families; several hundred souls have been touched by the love of God, in seven different countries. All from a twenty-five cents seed.

Those twenty-five cents were equivalent to 2500 dollars that some of you have—or don't have. For a few of you it would be 25000 dollars. Are you willing to let that go? Watch what God can do with that seed in the next five years. You may say, five years, that is a long period of time, I want something tomorrow. No, it doesn't work that way.

If you sow a seed, you need to wait for the harvest. Different seeds take different lengths of time to produce a harvest. The Bible says seed-time and harvest shall not cease (Genesis 8:22).

You may ask, how did God give me the money? God didn't send it on a string from heaven. He gave me ideas that I didn't have before, and I put those ideas into practice, and these produced my harvest. God gives ideas, and they are seeds; you need to find the ways to make them work.

If He has given you ideas, he will provide the amount you need miraculously to put that idea to work. What you need to do is to be in His presence, rather than running around to find it.

5) The Garden

The fifth thing that God gave to man when He created him was a garden. Genesis 2:8 says, "And the Lord God planted a garden eastward in Eden; and there he put the man whom He had formed."

God is a loving and caring Father. He prepared a place for the man to live and enjoy his life. It is impossible to imagine the luxury and beauty of the Garden of Eden. It was the best place we can imagine with our minds.

Eden was the house where Adam lived. God, who is his Father, prepared the best place on this earth for his son to live in. There was plenty of everything to eat and be healthy.

Adam didn't have to worry about what he was going to eat. God provided him with every imaginable fruit and vegetable, because he was God's son. God provided for His children in the wilderness and in both the Old and New Testaments.

If you are God's child, it is His responsibility to provide for you. This is why Jesus asked us to look at the birds and learn the lesson. They don't worry about their daily provision. He said, "Now if God so clothes the grass of the field, which today is, and tomorrow is thrown into the oven, will He not much more clothe you, O you of little faith" (Matthew 6:30).

God's will was done in Eden as it was in heaven. There is no sickness in heaven; so, there was no sickness, worry, or poverty in Eden. There is no death or murder in heaven; so, there was no death or murder in Eden. God's kingdom was established in Eden. That is what Jesus meant when He taught us to pray. He taught us to pray, "let His kingdom come, and His will be done on this earth as it is in heaven" (Matthew 6:10).

This means, the life that we would live in heaven should manifest here on earth. Jesus said, "I have come that they may have life, and they may have it more abundantly" (John 10: 10b).

Jesus came so that we can have life, not death or sickness, as some think in their weird minds. Paul said to the believers in Ephesians that they should be filled with all the fullness of God (Ephesians 3:19b).

In Thessalonians, he said that we should be blessed with all blessings and lacking nothing (1 Thessalonians 4:12). This is God's original desire for each of us, regardless of where we were born.

Adam had a house to live in before God brought the woman to him. He didn't have to worry about what they were going to eat and where they were going to stay after he was married.

Are you tired of trying to make a living by working yourself to death? Be a child of the Almighty God, and listen carefully to His voice. He has prepared everything for you, even before you were born.

Your house, food, wife or husband were all created together when God created you. God didn't just create your spirit, soul, and body. With that He has made all the things your spirit, soul, and body would ever need.

What kind of parents would we be if we just had a new-born baby and didn't have any clothes for the baby? Do you run to the store after you have the baby? God works the same way. When He made you, at the same time He prepared everything that you need.

The Bible says in Romans 8:32 "He who did not spare His own son, but delivered Him up for us all, how shall He not with Him also freely give us all things?" He has prepared the good works before the foundation of the earth for us to walk in it. (Ephesians 2:10).

6) Work

The sixth thing that God gave to man when He created him, was work. Genesis 2:15 says, "And the Lord God took the man, and put him in the Garden of Eden to tend and keep it." God gave him work or responsibility.

It was man's responsibility to keep the garden and to till and dress it. He had to work in order to keep the place clean and productive.

Do you see something, dear child of God? Adam was God's son, and He loved him so much and gave him everything according to His capacity. But He won't do what Adam can do.

It was Adam's work to keep the garden and farm it year after year. Many expect God to do what they are supposed to do—clean their bedroom, and wash their dishes, and keep their yard mowed and plants trimmed. No, that is not God's job. It is God's design for us to be responsible and take good care of everything that He has given us.

It is God's design for us to work. Many people think that if God loves them so much, He should get them out of work and let them stay home and be lazy. No, just the opposite is true. The more you love God and get close to Him, the more He trusts you with more responsibility. The more you know God and receive from Him, He expects you to give more so that He can give you more. That is a Kingdom principle. The Bible says to whom much is given much is required (Luke 12:48).

Your work is God-given, and you don't take a voluntary retirement from it. Your retirement is when you take your last breath. Otherwise, the work that you have is not from God. There is a difference between a job and work. A job is something temporary that you do until you find your work. Work is permanent, and it is God's purpose for your life.

You have been sent to this earth to accomplish a mission, and when you complete it, He will call you back home, and then you retire. We don't see anyone in the Bible retire when they are 55 or 65 years old. Their retirement was their death, and they died happy—not in a nursing home.

We live in a messed-up world, and every system in it works against Kingdom principles. I have seen precious people living disappointed when they have nothing to do or are tired of what they have been doing when they have reached age 60 or above.

Doing God's purpose is never boring, and you will be more joyful at the end than at the beginning. The Bible says, "The end of a thing is better than its beginning" (Ecclesiastes 7:8a).

7) The Word

The seventh thing that God gave to man when He created him was His Word. Genesis 2:16 and 17 says, "And the Lord God commanded the man, saying, 'Of every tree of the garden you may freely eat; but of the tree of the knowledge of good and evil, you shall not eat, for in the day that you eat of it you shall surely die.'"

Before God brought the woman to Adam, God gave him His Word—the most powerful weapon in the whole universe. The Word is the most powerfully creative force on the face of the earth. When God made Eve, He didn't tell her the second time what He told Adam.

It was Adam's responsibility to teach the Word that he received from God to his wife, Eve. I don't think he did a good job. Well, you know what happened; she told the serpent things that God didn't command Adam. Here, God is setting an order for all the families to follow. Man is the head of the woman, and he is the priest and the prophet in the family. He has to hear from God for his family, and not expect them to take care of themselves.

These days Adams are so busy taking care of the garden, they have no time to teach and train their families the Word of God. When we break God's order, we end up in a mess; and so we can't put the blame on God. That doesn't mean God never speaks to woman. History has proven that God uses women as well as men to build His Kingdom.

The first covenant God made with the Israelites when they came out of Egypt was a covenant of healing. In Exodus 15:26 (KJV) we read that, "If thou wilt diligently hearken to the voice of the LORD thy God, and wilt do that which is right in his sight, and wilt give ear to his commandments, and keep all his statutes, I will put none of these diseases upon thee, which I have brought upon the Egyptians: for I am the LORD that healeth thee."

Wow!! What a powerful promise! He told the people of Israel that when they reached the Promised Land, to keep and obey His Word so that no enemy would be a threat to them. When Joshua took over the leadership to lead His people to cross Jordan and do all the battles, God told Joshua the same thing.

We read in Joshua 1:5 (KJV) saying, "There shall not any man be able to stand before thee all the days of thy life: as I was with Moses, so I will be with thee; I will not fail thee, nor forsake thee." Verse eight says, "This book of the law shall not depart out of thy mouth; but thou shalt meditate therein day and night, that thou mayest observe to do according to all that is written therein: for then shalt make thy way prosperous, and then thou shalt have good success."

Psalm 1:2 & 3 (KJV) says, "But his delight is in the law of the LORD; and in his law doth he meditate day and night. And he shall be like a tree planted by the rivers of water, that bringeth forth his fruit in his season; his leaf also shall not wither; and whatsoever he doeth shall prosper."

Jesus said in John 15:7 (KJV), "If ye abide in me and my words abide in you, ye shall ask what ye will, and it shall be done unto you."

Many misunderstand when they hear the Word saying to meditate on it day and night. You may think, how can it be possible for anyone to meditate on the Word day and night?

I am sure; no one can sit before the Bible for all day and night. Please don't even attempt it; because that is not what it means. *Day and night* means that your life and thoughts are guided or governed by the Word of God.

When you are at work, driving or shopping wherever you are, your thoughts and imaginations are fixed in the anchor of the Word of God. The word *meditate* has to do with our minds; so, what God is saying, is to fill our minds with His Word so that any situation that arises in our lives, we will be bold enough to face it based on the principles of the Word of God. When the devil comes with a temptation and knocks at our door, the Word will answer the devil instead of our vulnerable flesh. He says, "Then we shall have good success."

You may ask, can it be possible for anyone to keep all that is written in sixty-six books of the Bible? No, you don't have to.

God is asking you and me to keep only two things. Love the Lord your God with all your heart and all your soul, and your neighbor as you love yourself. Do you think we can do this if we try? You don't have to kill a thousand sheep or jump twelve feet high or walk around the great wall of China seventy times.

The Bible says in 1 John 5:3, "For this is the love of God, that we keep His commandments: and his commandments are not grievous." When we keep the two commandments that Jesus gave us, all the rest of the Word of God is included in that.

8) The Woman

The eighth thing that God gave to man was a woman. Genesis 2:18 says, "And the LORD God said, "It is not good that man should be alone; I will make him a helper comparable to him." I ask audiences when I preach, "What has God given to man when He created him?" Most answer saying "woman."

Do you see why so many marriages are broken and many get wounded in their hearts? Statistics say the divorce rate in the church is higher than in the world. God had to prepare his son, Adam, before he brought the woman to him. Just because he was breathing and had a functioning body, he was not ready for marriage.

The purpose of marriage is not to have sex. If you are a single person who is reading this book, make sure your mate has all the qualities that God wants him or her to have in their lives.

Or if you are married, buy a copy of this book for someone who is planning to get married. Most do not think about these things when they are planning to get married. All the focus is on sex or what the flesh can give. God forbid that we bring reproach to His name among the heathen. Just because you have turned twenty or even thirty years of age, you are not necessarily ready to get married.

I will share with you at the end of this chapter about why God brought Eve to Adam; it was not for having sex alone.

Please make sure the person you are planning to marry knows his or her purpose. If you are a girl, make sure the guy you are planning to get married has found his work or purpose. If he hasn't, there is a very slight chance your marriage is going to be successful; and don't expect that he will go out and find a work after he is married. He will kiss you anywhere you want to if you let him stay home and just play CDs and "worship" and intercede for you. If you are a man, make sure the woman is willing to help you to fulfill God's purpose. It doesn't matter how cute she might look; she will make your life miserable otherwise.

When God brought Eve to Adam, he didn't have a second thought about the reason why God created her. He was already aware of his purpose in taking care of the garden, and it was too much for him to do it alone. So, God said, "It is not good for man to be alone. He needs a helper to assist him to do the task I have given the man."

Woman was brought to help the man fulfill God's purpose. Adam was given the Word of God, and it was his duty to teach the woman concerning her new surroundings. God didn't repeat His Word to the woman a second time. It was His design for the woman to work under man's leadership.

God didn't breathe the second time when He made the woman. The same spirit that was in man went into woman also. Though woman is not inferior in spirit to man, they both have different roles and different functions as long as they are on this earth

CHAPTER TWO

Seven Kinds of Believers

Since the fall of man, God in His mercy has been working in a non-stop attempt to restore what we lost. He has painted a beautiful picture in the book of Exodus for us to understand the process of salvation and redemption.

Salvation according to God is a whole-being experience. It is not just for the spirit, but includes the body and soul. Most believers do not experience salvation in their soul and body; as they limit it only to their spirit. Jesus didn't come to offer a partial salvation, rather he came to give us wholeness.

The church has been preaching the partial gospel—salvation limited to the spirit-man. When I was seeking God in this regard, the Holy Spirit revealed to me that it is possible for all believers to receive the total package.

The Old Testament is a shadow of things that are revealed in the New Testament. The exodus of the Israelites from Egypt is a shadow of our salvation that we receive through Christ Jesus.

When we study the book of Exodus from the time Moses went to Egypt to tell the Pharaoh to let the people of God go, we see that

Pharaoh loses his grip step by step. It was not an at once incident; it took a series of incidents and time to release God's people.

Each time God sent His judgment or plagues, Pharaoh's grip was diminished. He offered them various options, but Moses was not willing to accept anything less than the total salvation of God's people from Egypt. I call it the God-kind of salvation. That is what He has in store for each of us, and if we persist enough, we can have everything that God promised to us.

There are seven steps we see in the book of Exodus that the people of God went through before they were redeemed from Egypt. Each step shows different levels of spiritual life where people choose to live their lives.

It is up to us which level we choose. We are going to look in detail and learn how we can receive the best God has for us.

After I mention each "kind," I have added the revelation we need in order to go to the next level. It is my prayer that we all reach the level of seventh kind of believer, who inherits the promises of God with faith and patience.

7 KINDS OF BELIEVERS

First Kind
Saved, but Trapped in Egypt

When God sent Moses into Egypt to deliver His people, Pharaoh was not willing to let the people go. God began to send plagues to Egypt; then Pharaoh called Moses and said, "Go ye, sacrifice to your God in the land." Exodus 8:25 (KJV). But that was not God's plan for His people. God's plan for His people was to go three days journey into the wilderness and there offer sacrifices to the Lord.

Moses said, "It is not meet so to do; for we shall sacrifice the abomination of the Egyptians to the LORD our God; lo, shall we sacrifice the abomination on the Egyptians before their eyes, then will they not stone us?" (Exodus 8:26). So, Moses refused his suggestion and began to fight again for freedom.

Sadly, today, some accept this as an opportunity. They think at least now they can worship God and not remain in spiritual bondage. They think salvation means only to worship God and offer sacrifices.

Their salvation experience ends as soon as they finish worship and their spirit gets saved. They are saved, but still remain in Egypt. Their health, wealth, family, children, destiny are bound by Pharaoh. They are not free to fulfill the call of God.

This group does not know what the purpose of God is for their lives. Though they are saved, their outward life does not show or reflect God's saving grace. The enemy has made them believe that all blessings of the earth are evil. We are supposed to live as poor as we can so that we can inherit a better place in heaven. However, 3 John 2 says, we need to prosper and be in good health as our soul prospers.

These believers will teach you that if you are truly spiritual, you will live like Jesus lived. They will have an outward appearance of godliness but will not have the power Jesus had in His life. They believe the more afflicted and poorer they are on this side of heaven, the greater their reward and will be in heaven.

They are not helping God's Kingdom, and they don't have anything to contribute to this earth or God's kingdom for they have nothing to give, they are just passing by to glory. They accept every evil as the will of God. If they get sick, they will say God is making them more holy. They are helping the devil to build his kingdom of darkness. Because they are not receiving what God has prepared for them, the devil has that much more to use.

These people have a demon of tradition and a form of spirituality. They will appear to be poor and ascetic in their outward expressions. Their spiritual lives will never grow any further than their salvation experience. They cannot grow because they have limited God only to the salvation of their spirit. They will be praying the same spiritual prayers and singing the same old hymns, and always having a good story about what God has done in the past.

They have a past-God and a future-God, but nothing for the present. God has done mighty things in the past, and He is going to do more in the future, but He will not do anything right now because it is not His time. Have you ever met anyone like this in your life?

They still receive scourging and torture from their taskmasters because they are still in Egypt. They believe it is God who sends such trials to teach them His ways. They are still under slavery, poor, and tormented. They get sick, and some die of it, believing it was God's will for that to happen to them.

Imagine what would have happened to the people of Israel if Moses agreed to Pharaoh's suggestion to remain in Egypt?

For them, life on earth is boring and non-exciting because the earth is evil and all that is in it belongs to the devil. That is what the Israelites thought when they were in Egypt. They had no life beyond what Pharaoh had let them live. He decided what they could have and where they could go. They didn't have the freedom to make choices. Pharaoh made decisions for them.

There are millions of Christians who are satisfied with the salvation of their spirit, and do not experience any freedom in their souls or bodies. They have been deceived by the enemy. Their lives reflect as if Jesus didn't do a good job on the cross. They think there still remains a price to be paid, and Satan needs to be defeated if they are to have total freedom.

Dear child of God, you don't have to remain in Egypt. Egypt is a land of lack, bondage, sin, and a curse. This group believes that they have to live with those things because they are not able to overcome them on this earth. They have accepted their lifestyle as if it were God's will for their lives.

They blame the devil for every trouble they face. They are open to his attack because they have not yet moved out of his domain. They have not submitted to the Lordship of Jesus Christ though they may say it with their mouths. Though they come to church to worship, they have not really overcome sin.

Egypt represents the dominion of sin. The Bible says sin will not have dominion over us because we are not under the law (Romans 6:14).

Egypt is comfortable for them because they have not moved into God's kingdom or destiny. They will not fulfill God's destiny, because no one can fulfill their God-given destiny while remaining a slave to Pharaoh. Dear Child of God, do you think the devil is your problem? Then, please, move out of Egypt.

They will say we are also worshipping God, and we will go to heaven when we die. Not so; the Christian life was never meant to be a miserable one! The yoke that Christ gives is *easy*, and His burden is *light*. If the burden you have is unbearable, that is not from Christ (Matthew 11 :29).

You might be put in prison, but if you are a Christian you can rejoice. Though you walk through the valley of the shadow of death, you will fear no evil. God's goodness and mercy shall follow you all the days of your life.

This group has no control over their lives. They will not accept anything different because they are programmed with an *Egyptian* mentality. Most of their songs will be about death and life after death.

It is time for us to open our eyes and see the redemption that God offered us through Christ Jesus.

These people remind me of the nature of the brother of the prodigal son in Luke chapter fifteen. Though he was living in his father's house, he never enjoyed any of the blessings. He never understood the potential and resources that were made available to him by his father.

In the next chapter we are going to see from his life why people resist becoming everything God has made them to be.

CHAPTER 3

The Brother of the Prodigal

The brother of the prodigal son reminds me of many Christians today. He was working hard with the servants of his father. I believe he got the same wage as the servants. The bottom line was, there were seemingly no difference between him and the servants; the only difference might have been that he slept in his father's house.

He didn't have any idea of what he was entitled to. He didn't know what he owned. He had spent many of the years of his life toiling in the sun to earn a few dollars.

Please don't misunderstand me. I am not against hard-working people. Work is God's design, and He expects us to work. But there is a difference between working harder and working smarter.

When the prodigal son came back to his father, the father ordered his servants to arrange a great celebration with music and dance. The brother of the prodigal heard the sound of music as he was coming from the field and inquired about all the strange happenings at home.

He was told the story, and his face turned red. He ran to his father to present his case. He was working all day long in the field day in and day out. He complained to his father that what he was doing was not right. His complaint was genuine but from an ignorant heart. He said that his father didn't let him have even a "skinny goat" to celebrate with his friends.

The answer of the father is one of my favorite verses in the Bible. He said, "Son, you are always with me, and all that I have is yours" (Luke 15: 31).

The eldest son had a preconceived idea about his father's character. He didn't know his father and his intent. He didn't know that what his father owned was his.

He misunderstood his father. Maybe it was based on a childhood experience, he may have concluded that his father would not give him anything to enjoy. His father might not have granted him what he asked for when he was a child because his father knew he was not of age to handle it. So perhaps the son built a "mindset" around that one incident and began thinking, "I won't ask anything of my father, because he won't give me any good things." Instead his father may have been protecting him from getting his life destroyed.

I have seen many Christians like that; they asked something from God, and because He didn't give it to them, they thought that God would never give them any good things. They think that God is being mean to them so they have to go out and get their own stuff.

I know a couple of people who prayed for a mate, and God didn't send the person when they wanted. So, they started sleeping with anyone they could find, and ended up in more of a mess than at the beginning. They didn't really want a "mate" because a mate would bring responsibility; what they wanted was "free sex."

We are going to look in detail at some of the differences between these two sons in Luke Chapter fifteen. 1 found some interesting but profound thoughts from their natures that would help us know what we can become in Christ.

1) The elder brother was ignorant, and didn't know how to utilize his father's possessions

He knew his father had fatted calves and never bothered to ask the purpose of them. He didn't know he could have it to celebrate with his friends. The Bible says, "For every beast of the forest is mine, and the cattle on a thousand hills" (Psalm 50:10).

Have you lately asked him, what is their purpose? He knew his father had musicians and dancers, but he never thought he could have enjoyed any of them.

He woke up every morning, went to work in the field with the servants of his father and was living on daily wages. I have heard of children of corporate giants, hesitating to take over their father's business. They think if they do that, it would make them a "wimp" to receive it from their father. They think they have something to "prove," and end up in the gutters with drugs and prostitutes. Don't be a rascal, but rather be a son.

Solomon became what he was because he received instruction and wealth from his father, David. Without David, Solomon wouldn't have become what he became. He received the instruction to get wisdom and fear of the Lord from David. Proverbs 2:3,4 and Psalm 34:10.

2) The elder brother thought that he had to work hard to earn something from his father

Romans 8:32 says, "He who did not spare His own son, but delivered him up for us all, how shall he not with him also freely give us all things." God gives us blessings not because we deserve it, but because He loves us. The Bible says, "Who has first given God anything that he might be paid back or that he could claim a recompense?" (Romans 11: 35 AMB).

We cannot earn the grace of God, but we can receive the grace of God. I have seen many Christians working hard like a racehorse to get something that already belonged to them. I was one of them.

The older son never took a moment to talk with his father and spend some time with him learning to know his heart. He was busy working like a slave to earn a few dollars when he could have owned the business.

Many do not believe that this earth belongs to God. They think the devil has more authority on this earth than God himself. The Bible says the earth and its fullness belongs to the lord (Psalm 24:1).

Let me tell you the good news; the devil cannot move his little finger without God's permission. What we do need is more time in His presence, not a new idea or more money.

The world looked at the first century disciples and said, "They realized that they had been with Jesus" (Acts 4:13b). That is what made the difference, and I believe that is the only thing that is going to help us win this world for Him. The early church turned their cities upside down for Jesus, and today cities turn churches upside down with their new laws and regulations.

3) The elder brother was not ready to let go of his ego to receive something for free

Do you know why many do not accept Christ and His salvation? Because He offers it for free. The entire world knows that Jesus was a nice person, and they know He died on the cross and rose again. But they can't let go of their pride and the "I can do it myself" syndrome in order to come to Him and receive eternal life.

If God offered salvation on the basis of money or status, there would have been more "nice" Christians on the face of this earth today. The Bible says, "God has chosen the foolish things of the world to put to shame the wise, and God has chosen the weak things of the world to put to shame the things which are mighty" (1 Corinthians 1:27).

Whatever you receive from God is a free gift. You might ask, "Didn't you fast and pray, or give a thousand dollars to so and so?" Whatever you have, is a gift from God. What about those non-Christians in the world who are more blessed than many Christians, how did they get blessed? They didn't fast and pray to receive a breakthrough. They spent their nights in clubs and bars. God blessed them because He loves them, and He is love. We pray and fast not to change Him, but to show our dependency on Him and to be changed into His image and likeness.

4) The elder brother was willing only to receive according to his own capacity, not his father's capacity to give

He was not willing to explore the blessings of his father. He limited himself by depending on his ability to achieve instead of partnering with his father. Many believe for things that only fit and can be worked out in their minds. Your God is bigger than your mind.

Many are carnally-minded; if their flesh is not comfortable, they won't try to do anything. They always think based on their body, and not their spirit. His desire was only as big as both his hands could hold. Many do not have what God can do through them. Many limits God based on their mental understanding of Him. God is unlimited, and whatever He has is unlimited.

We cannot fit God into a box, and our mind is a box. Human minds can never comprehend the immensity of God. Many do not fulfill their dream or purpose because they think their dream is too big to be achieved.

Man is incapable of dreaming of things he thinks cannot be achieved. You have the ability to dream and also the ability to fulfill that dream. Five hundred years ago, no one ever thought man could go to the moon. They thought that was an impossible dream. You and I know what happened; someone decided that it could happen, and they made it happen.

You cannot see something that does not exist. That is the number one principle of vision. You can see things in the spirit, though it may not be visible in the natural realm, but it has the potential to manifest in the natural realm.

We have two different kinds of sight; natural sight and spiritual sight. Natural eyes see things that are only visible to the natural eyes. If you can see something with your natural eyes it exists in the natural realm, and if you see something with your spiritual eyes it exists in the spiritual realm. They both are real and necessary for a productive living.

Many do not believe the dreams that come to them have any potential to be accomplished so they ignore them as mere thoughts. These are not just man's thoughts; they are glimpses of what is eternal. The Bible says, "... For the things which are seen are temporary, but the things which are not seen are eternal" (2 Corinthians 4:18b).

God gave us our natural eyes to see and our spiritual eyes to dream. Some do the opposite; they dream only things that their natural eyes can see. That is not a dream but a wish. When you see something, you say, I wish I had it. The Bible says, "... We walk by faith, not by sight" (2 Corinthians 5:7).

We are never supposed to be led by our sight or natural eyes, only by faith—the vision of the spiritual eyes. I usually say this to myself and others: When you plan to do something, do not plan based on what you have, but according to what God has. Jeremiah 32:27 says, "... Is there anything too hard for me?"

5) The elder brother was not willing to ask and receive

He lived with his father all his life, but he never asked his father for something. How do I know that? If that was not the case, his father wouldn't have said what he said, "Son, you are always with me, and all that I have is yours" (Luke 15:31). Many think if God knows everything before you ask, then why should you pray and ask? Jesus said, "Our Father knows what we need before we ask Him" (Matthew 6:8).

If God sent his son to this earth, didn't he know everything His son ever needed? If that is so, then why did Jesus spend most of His nights in prayer? If you think you are too smart to pray, then you are truly smarter than God. You should try to create another heaven and earth, and let me know when that happens.

There are four reasons why people do not ask God for help:

The first one is they don't want to humble themselves to show that they need help. They would rather die in their pride being miserable.

Second, they are too content with what they have and are not willing to become productive. They are selfish and do not want to be a blessing to someone else.

The third reason people do not ask, is because they are afraid that God may get angry at them for asking big things. This brother might have thought, "If I ask my father for more than the wages I get, what if he gets upset and fires me from my job."

The fourth reason people do not ask God, is some believe if God wants them to have something, He would just give it to them whether they ask or not.

The Bible says, "... Yet you do not have because you do not ask" (James 4:2b). Jesus said, "Ask, and it shall be given to you" (Matthew

7:7a). Many are good at praying a bless me or bless them prayers. They have been doing that since childhood and every day saying "Father, bless Mummy, bless Daddy, bless Rachel, bless Grandpa and Grandma. Jesus name Amen." Very few know how to ask specifically and receive specific answers.

One thing I see in the Gospels is that when people came to Jesus to receive a miracle, He was not willing to help them unless they were specific about their need. No one came to Jesus and just said, "Lord bless me" and received a blessing. Do you see what I see, dear child of God? The blind man came to Him for help; he cried out by saying, "Jesus, son of David, have mercy on me" (Mark 10:47).

It was obvious that he was blind; Jesus or anyone could see that he was blind. Jesus asked him, "What do you want me to do for you?" Jesus was willing to show him mercy but wanted him to express which area of his life needed God's mercy. The blind man was not specific in his request. The Bible says, "You ask and do not receive, because you ask amiss ..." (James 4:3).

6) The older brother lived for the present and had no future goals

He couldn't think beyond himself. He thought he was the best, and his brother was an outcast. He probably thought, "Because my brother is messed up, he is no longer worthy to have the same things that I have. He should not be loved the same way I am qualified to be loved. I am more holy and superior to my brother, because I didn't commit the sins that he did.

The Bible says, "Where there is no vision the people perish" (Proverbs 29:18a AMB).

Vision gives you passion and meaning to your life. Vision gives you hunger for more of God. Vision gives you motivation to live.

Many think if God wants them to do something, He will make them do it because He is God.

Did you comb your head this morning? You did it not because God made you do it, but you know it has to be done. God does not comb anyone's hair. How do you know you have to change your clothes when it gets dirty? God doesn't need to tell you to change your clothes. God will not do anything significant on this earth unless someone asks Him.

Otherwise, the father would have given him a calf to celebrate with his friends. He had a desire in his heart to enjoy his life with his friends. God puts a desire in your heart, and it is your responsibility to act upon it. Jesus could have made any of His disciples to walk on the water, but He told only to Peter to come because Peter asked Him. He was willing to step out.

This son was concerned about his survival. H. Drummond said, "Unless a man undertakes more than he possibly can do, he will never do all he can do. "The only difference between Joseph and his brothers was a "dream."

7) He was the older son, but he acted and lived like a servant

His father couldn't help him, because of his servant mentality. I believe he voluntarily joined the servants to work for his father. He received wages like the servants received. I don't think his father would have asked him to work in the field.

The Bible says in Galatians 4:1 "Now I say the heir, as long as he is a child, does not differ at all from a slave though he is master of all." Do we act like servants or sons of God on this earth? I believe we have more servants than sons.

Servants do not get treated as sons. If you are a son of God, act like one. We should have the attitude of a son, but the heart of a servant. Many have the attitude of a servant and do not have the heart.

The Bible says in John 1:12 "But as many as received Him, to them He gave the right to become children of God." Jesus said to his disciples, "No longer do I call you servants, ...But I have called you friends" (John 15:15). Luke 3:38b says, "Adam was the son of God."

God will not force His blessings upon us. He says clearly in His Word who we are and what we can have. It is our responsibility to find it out and act upon it. Though we may serve God, we are not mere servants and He deals with us as His sons. Do we live like a son or a like a servant?

It is a mystery to me why his father never took him aside and explained to him what he could have. Have you ever thought that you wish God would appear in front of you and explain to you who you are and what you can do? To my understanding He will not. Why? Because whatever we need to know is explained in His Word. I have seen people with false humility not accepting the position that God has presented to them.

8) The older brother was waiting for that perfect "day"

He knew someday he was going to have more than what he had. He knew his father would divide the inheritance between him and his brother. Many are waiting to get to heaven in order to receive what they are supposed to have on earth. He didn't think he could have anything "now" and enjoy his father's blessings. His father didn't say to him, "Son, whatever is mine is going to be yours." Instead he said it belonged to him right now. It was not his "vision" that made him wait for what he could have now, but ignorance.

I have seen many dear saints of God who are sick in their bodies willing to wait to get to heaven in order to be healed. Healing is available now to whoever is in need. Jesus didn't die on the cross so that you could be healed in heaven. He died so that you could have it now. Let us shake off our religion and receive the truth of the Word of God. Many Christians believe in a futuristic gospel. Either things were better in the past or going to be better in the future; right now, you just have to put up with the mess.

The Bible says, "Jesus Christ is the same yesterday, today and forever" (Hebrews 13:8). The Bible says," Now faith is ..." (Hebrews 11:1a). Faith is now, or it is not faith but hope. Eternal life doesn't start after we die. If it were so, it would not be eternal. Eternal means without beginning or end, it is everlasting.

We were in God before the foundation of the earth, and we will live with Him forever and ever. Or else, how could He choose us before the foundation of the earth? Jesus taught us to pray for His will to be done on this earth as it is in heaven.

9) The older brother's attitude was that if he couldn't have it now, no one else should either

He was jealous of seeing his brother getting blessed. I believe he had a religious spirit in him thinking that his brother was no longer worthy to receive his father's love. He thought that if you messed up once, you were done forever.

Through this parable, Jesus was showing the difference between two different dispensations. These are the dispensation of law and the dispensation of grace. The brother of the prodigal son shows righteousness through good works, and the prodigal son shows the free gift of God.

Sadly, there are many who believe today that righteousness is based on their good works. They think they are little more holy than the others because they have not messed up as much as someone else has.

Under the Old Testament law, the prodigal son couldn't be forgiven without any punishment. The brother was expecting that at least the father would rebuke him, keep him outside for two days, make him work with the servants; and not accept back him as a son that quick. He didn't understand his father's love. God's love is not conditional. The Bible says He loved us while we were sinners (Romans 5:8).

The prodigal's brother was trying to earn his father's love through hard work, but he missed it. He may have thought—now that my brother has gone with what belongs to him, and so what is left, is going to be mine.

Do we think something similar in our lives? Are we trying to earn God's love, or are we accepting it freely as much as we accept the unconditional love of God; and even more challenging, is to give that same love to others.

The Bible says, "... That the world may know that You have sent Me, and have loved them as you have loved Me" (John 17:23b; 15:9).

We don't have to remain in Egypt. Provision has been made for us to enjoy life in full. The only thing we need to do is to adjust our mindset and believe the Word of God.

We don't need to worship our God in Egypt. God wants us to worship Him in Spirit and in truth. Wherever the Spirit of the Lord is, there is freedom; and, the only thing that can lead us to that freedom, is the truth of God's Word.

7 KINDS OF BELIEVERS

Second Kind
Saved, but Often Takes Trips Back to Egypt

Three | The Brother of the Prodigal

As God sent plagues again, Pharaoh began to loosen his grip little by little. He said you go out of Egypt but not too far. Exodus 8:28 (KJV) says, "And pharaoh said, I will let you go, that ye may sacrifice to the LORD your God in the wildness; only ye shall not go very far away."

These are the mediocre group. They go out of Egypt to worship God, but return to the same place afterwards. They are like rubber bands. As long as they are under the anointing of the visiting preacher, they will dance and shout. When the preacher leaves town, they shrink back to their original position.

They have no root in the Word and no active relationship with God. They don't learn anything from the Word. They seem genuine and open to receive the things of God but don't retain what they have learned. They will travel from Egypt any distance in order to attend a spiritual warfare conference.

They are fighting the same enemy for a lifetime, but don't seem to get anywhere. They don't believe they can have total victory over the devil in this life. Their theology is, you just need to accept what life brings because if you try to fight the enemy for freedom, "what if the devil gets mad and does something destructive?" They believe the enemy is too strong for them to overcome. They won't go for the best in life, but only accept what comes normally. If you accept only what comes normally to your life, nothing much will come.

They want the respect of both the church and the world. One foot is in the church and the other in the world. They are good politicians. When they are in church, they will put on sheep's clothing, and when they leave the church they will put on the wolf's skin. They know the talk of the world and the common church phrases that show their spirituality. Inside their heart, they know they are barren and empty.

WWW.THEKINGDOMNETWORK.ORG

Dear child of God, God loves us and paid the highest price to redeem us. We are His children. Stop blaming the devil for your problems. The devil is doing his job that God appointed him to do.

No church in this world or no great Apostle is ever going to bind all the demons on this earth. They are left here for a reason. Just like the cops are appointed by the state to discipline those who break the laws, the devil is appointed by God to torment those who break the laws of God.

The Bible says we cannot serve two masters. We will love one and hate the other. We cannot love God and mammon (Matthew 6:24). In 1 John 2:15, it says if anyone loves the world and its things, the love of the Father is not in him. This group is lukewarm and cannot make any difference for God on this earth. They want both Egypt and the Promised Land.

Their lives are like rowing a boat that has been tied to the tree. Their minds are not renewed with the Word of God. Many times, they still get upset with their past. They dig out what Christ has buried. The roots of their problems have not healed. Their deliverance is temporary. They can't forget Egypt because they didn't have to walk by faith in Egypt.

The journey to the Promised Land is a walk of faith. We don't know where our provision for tomorrow comes from. In Egypt, even though it was cucumber and garlic, they knew for sure they were going to be provided for. They don't want to leave their whole life to the Lord. They like to be in control of their lives. This is the main reason they don't want to leave Egypt forever. Jesus said if any man loves his life, he will lose it; but if he loses his life for the sake of the kingdom, he will find it (Mark 8:35).

The reason why this group remains where they are, is because they don't have a clear picture of redemption through Jesus Christ.

They don't understand the position, power, and privilege God has given to them for free.

When the prodigal son came back, his father arranged a very unique "reception" ceremony. He gave him certain things that shed light for us to understand our redemption.

The father gave him five material things that we are going to explore so that we don't have to go back to Egypt anymore. We can move forward in the wilderness journey to inherit our Promised Land.

CHAPTER FOUR

The Blessing of the Prodigal

God doesn't waste His time; He does not mention anything in His Word without a reason. We are going to see now why the father of the prodigal received his son the way he received him.

I believe Jesus shared the parable of the prodigal son to show us a picture of the redemption that was going to be revealed through Him. He wants us to know the unconditional love the Father has for His children.

There are powerful spiritual truths hidden in each of the things that were given to him when he returned. The Bible says in Luke 15:20, 22-24 (KJV), "And he arose and came to his father, But when he was yet a great way off, his father saw him and had compassion, and ran and fell on his neck, and kissed him … but the father said to his servants, 'Bring out the best robe and put it on him, and put a ring on his hand, and shoes on his feet; and bring hither the fatted half and kill it; and let us eat and be merry: For this my son was dead, and is alive again: he was lost, and is found, And they began to be merry."

These are the five things the father had given to his son:

1) He kissed him

2) He gave him the best robe

3) He gave him a ring

4) He gave him shoes

5) He killed the fatted calf

We are going to look in detail at what each of these things signifies to us in our lives. I believe Jesus used this parable to show us the heart of the Father.

God is the most misunderstood person in the entire universe. Imagine what a picture people would have of God if they knew only the Old Testament? I still have some difficulty accepting God's unconditional love myself. Maybe this is because I didn't really receive that kind of love from anyone on this earth when I was a child. Jesus said he came to reveal the Father (John 1:18).

1) He kissed him

> The Bible says in Luke 15:20, that "... his father saw him, and had compassion, and ran and fell on his neck and kissed him."
>
> This shows the acceptance of his father. The father had been waiting for the return of his son. When he saw him, he ran to receive him. He passionately expressed his love.
>
> It was not mere words of "I love you" from his lips, but it was from his heart. His heart was open to receive him at any time.

The prodigal never expected his father to receive him that way. We don't see him accusing his son, or rebuking him for his bad behavior or for what he did. He just was happy that he got him back alive. Can you imagine having a father with such a heart?

He kissed him. This shows an intimate relationship. You greet someone with a kiss who is close to you. You greet someone with a kiss whom you trust. You greet someone with a kiss who you really love.

He may have been wearing shabby clothes and not taken a shower for days, yet that didn't keep the father from hugging and receiving his son. The heart of our Heavenly Father is open to receive anyone who comes to Him. He will never cast anyone away (John 6:37).

2) He gave him the best robe

The Bible says in Luke 15:22, "But the father said to his servants, 'Bring forth the best robe, and put it on him;'"

The robe represents righteousness. He told his servants to bring the best robe. How can you put the best robe on a prodigal son?

In different cultures you recognize the status of people by seeing what they wear. In different government offices we recognize the responsibility of a person by seeing their uniforms.

The Bible says our righteousness is like filthy rags before God (Isaiah 64:6). No one can stand before a Holy God with his own good works or self-righteousness. When we come to Christ, He exchanges his righteousness for our filthy rags. His righteousness is the best robe. There is no other best robe that you and I can put on other than the free gift of righteousness from Jesus.

Robes in the Old Testament

In the Old Testament, kings put their robes on people whom they honored or promoted into a higher position. If someone wears the King's robe, that means he is very close to the king. All the citizens of that country must respect that person as they respect the king. He is equal to the king in authority, but not in position.

In Genesis 41:43 & 44 (KJV), scripture says, "And he made him to ride in the second chariot which he had; and they cried before him, Bow the knee: and he made him ruler over all the land of Egypt. And Pharaoh said unto Joseph, I am Pharaoh, and without thee shall no man lift up his hand or foot in all the land of Egypt."

Esther 6:6-9 (KJV) says, "And the king said unto him, What shall be done unto the man whom the king delighteth to honour? ... And Haman answered the king, 'For the man whom the king delighteth to honor, Let the royal apparel be brought which the king useth to wear, and the horse that the king rideth upon, and the crown royal is set upon his head.'"

In Genesis 41:42 (KJV), the Bible says, "And Pharaoh took off his ring from his hand, and put it upon Joseph's hand, and arrayed him in vestures of linen, and put a gold chain about his neck."

Biblical Meaning

When God accepts us into His family He gives us His best robe. We can't enter his kingdom with our own earthly robe. On the cross Christ gave us His robe of righteousness, and He bore our filthy rags.

In Isaiah 61:10 (KJV), the Bible says, "I will greatly rejoice in the Lord; my soul shall be joyful in my God: for he hath clothed me with the garments of salvation, he hath covered me with the robe of righteousness …"

Jacob made a coat of many colors for his favorite son, Joseph. We must know our position in Christ in order to be effective for the Kingdom. Many do not understand their position. The Bible says, "And raised us up together, and made us sit together in the heavenly places in Christ Jesus" (Ephesians 2:6).

We have been seated in Christ Jesus in the heavenly places. Christ is the King of all kings, and heaven is God's throne. Ordinary people do not get to sit next to kings or his throne. Only dignitaries and royals receive such a privilege.

We have been made the children of the living God. Whosoever believes in the name of Jesus, God has given the power to become a son of God. Our position gives us power and authority. God has put the best robe on us and accepted us into His family.

Although the son came back thinking his father would treat him as a servant, the father accepted him as his dear son. He restored his position as his son. Let us believe the work of God, and thus see ourselves as He sees us.

3) He gave him a ring

The Bible says in Luke 15:22, "But the father said to servants.......put a ring on his hand..."

The ring in the Old Testament represents authority and position. In the Bible days, the kings used their ring as a symbol of power and authority. They gave a ring to a person to show that they delegated power and promoted a person to higher authority.

We read in Genesis 41:40-42 that when Pharaoh promoted Joseph as the top official in Egypt, he gave his ring to Joseph. "Thou shall be over my house, and according unto thy word shall all my people be ruled: only in the throne will I be greater than thou. And pharaoh said unto Joseph, See, I have set thee over all the land of Egypt. And Pharaoh took off his ring from his hand, and put it upon Joseph's hand ..." They also used their ring to seal their decrees and documents.

In Persia, if they sealed documents with their signet ring, it meant it was irrevocable. Esther 3:10 and 12 says, "And the king took his ring from his hand, and gave it unto Haman the son of Hammeda the Agagite, the Jew's enemy. Then were the king's scribes called on the thirteenth day of first month, and there was written according to all that Haman had commanded ... in the name of king Ahasuerus was it written, and sealed with the King's ring.

Esther 8:8 says, "Write ye also for the Jews, as it liketh you, in the king's name, and seal it with the king's ring: for the writing which is written in the king's name, and sealed with the king's ring, may no man reverse."

The father of the prodigal gave him a ring and restored his authority and position in the house, and made him a steward of everything he owned. The servants in his house did not receive a robe or a ring. This meant he could function once again as he used to before he went away as a prodigal.

Through redemption, God restored us back as His sons as Adam was in the beginning. We are made joint heirs with Christ to every heavenly inheritance and riches. Whatever Christ owns, we are given an equal ownership (Romans 8:17).

4) He gave him shoes

The Bible says in Luke 15:22, "But the father said to his servants … put a ring on his hand, and shoes on his feet:"

Shoes represent our inheritance. In an eastern culture, you recognize a person's position by his shoes. The king and rich people had special shoes that were made just for them. Shoes show inheritance. God told Joshua that every place the sole of your foot treads shall belong to you (Joshua 1:3).

Another custom in the Old Testament was that in redeeming properties or people, the practice involved the parties exchanging their shoes. Ruth 4:7 says, "Now this was the manner in former times in Israel concerning redeeming and concerning exchanging, to confirm all things: a man plucked off his shoe, and gave it to his neighbor: and this was a testimony in Israel."

The father gave his prodigal son shoes, confirming that he was legally entitled to everything his father owned. The father was making a legal heir. He was redeeming his son. He was doing all these symbolic gestures in order to assure his son that he really loved and accepted him.

The son had come with great doubts in his heart that his father would accept him. So, the father used what had been practiced traditionally for his son to know that he really meant what he said.

What if God had said that He loved us, without giving us His son, Jesus? We would not have accepted His love. However, the love and sacrifice of Jesus on the cross for us, left us without another choice, except to believe in God's love for us.

If you are a child of God, you have an inheritance. Jesus said the meek shall inherit the earth (Matthew 5:5). Kings used to divide their inheritance for their children. Jesus is the King of kings, and He has an inheritance for you on this earth, and in the earth to come.

Ephesians 1:18 says, "The eyes of your understanding being enlightened; that you may know what is the hope of His calling, and what are the riches of the glory of his inheritance in the saints."

5) He killed the fatted calf

The Bible says in Luke 15:23, "And bring hither the fatted calf, and kill it; and let us eat, and be merry."

The fatted calf shows the benefits and blessings. The fatted calf is kept for dignitaries and special guests. For ordinary meals, they don't kill the fatted calf. Again, the father is trying to prove to his son that he is special and his love for him is genuine.

Many doubt God's great love for them. They think it is too good to be true. They think why should God love them, when they live a life that is not pleasing to Him?

Others think if God loves me so much, why am I going through all these hardships?

God said that all the cattle on a thousand hills belong to Him. Does anyone know why He has all those cattle? He will satisfy us with the finest of the wheat (Psalm 81:16). He wants to satisfy our mouth with good things so that our youth is renewed like an eagle (Psalm 103:5).

God gave the children of Israel a land that flows with milk and honey. How long shall we be content with the least and the lean? Let us explore the storehouse of heaven. Let us have faith to receive the very best that God has for us.

7 KINDS OF BELIEVERS

Third Kind
Only Men and Children are Saved

After the seventh plague, Pharaoh called Moses and asked him who the people were who should go and serve his God? Exodus 10:8 (KJV) says, "Go serve your LORD your God; but who are they that shall go?" Moses said in verse nine, "We will go with our young and with our old, with our sons and with our daughters, with our flocks and with our herds will we go; for we must hold a feast unto the LORD." But Pharaoh said, only the men and children should go and worship the LORD; the women and rest of the stuff should remain in Egypt.

I have seen many families with only half of them serving the Lord. The husband is saved, but the wife is not saved. The husband is the leader and elder in the church, but the wife is doing her own thing. In some families, the husband and wife are saved, but the children are not saved. In other families the children are saved, but the parents are out serving the devil.

God's desire is that every aspect of our lives should experience redemption. We don't have to accept a partial salvation. It is God's will that our entire family be saved and blessed.

Pharaoh changed his mind yet again, and said only men should go to worship the Lord. In verse eleven we read, "Not so, go now ye that are men, and serve the LORD; for that ye did desire."

The Bible says in Acts 16:31, "Believe on the Lord Jesus Christ, and you will be saved, you and your household." Please don't give up fighting the Pharaoh for the salvation of your entire household. He has to let go of God's children to worship God.

Just because they are in Egypt, they don't belong there. They are supposed to be worshiping and serving God.

Have you ever thought about the people in this world today? God has made every life on this earth. Most do not know Him nor serve Him. Why? Because Pharaoh, the lord of this world, has kept them captive, and no one is there to fight for them as Moses did.

The devil didn't create a single soul that is alive on this earth today. Most Christians are playing safe and happy about their salvation. They are not ready to risk their lives to save someone.

We act selfishly as if we think that the unsaved are supposed to remain unsaved. May the Lord give us the heart of Moses to continue the fight so that all God's children may come home! The Bible says it is the Lord's desire that none should perish (Matthew 18:14).

If we need to move into a level where we will see all our household saved, we need to understand the laws that govern the spirit world.

Most of the time, family members remain unsaved, because we are so caught up with what we see in the natural, and then we draw a conclusion based on what we saw. We need to understand how the spirit world operates in order to receive the miracle we need.

Because of the fall, we lost the capacity to function as spiritual beings. Salvation is a spiritual blessing. This leads us to the next chapter, to understand clearly what spiritual blessings are all about.

CHAPTER FIVE

Spiritual Blessings

Ephesians 1:3 says, "Blessed be the God and Father of our Lord Jesus Christ, who has blessed us with every spiritual blessing in the heavenly places in Christ."

What are these spiritual blessings? How can one receive those blessings?

God didn't say He has blessed some or an elected few with spiritual blessings. Apostle Paul was writing to all the saints in Ephesus—not to just a few. I believe these are available to anyone who needs and seeks them.

When people think of spiritual blessings, they usually misunderstand:

> As I was preaching, I asked my team in India to mention some of the spiritual blessings. They said peace, joy, tongues, prophecy, salvation, healing, etc.
>
> All they could think of when they heard of "spiritual blessings" were things that were not tangible or concrete.

The apostle Paul was not talking about such things here. If we compare this scripture with others, and study it together with the help of the Holy Spirit, the scripture above says that God has blessed us with "every spiritual blessing."

We live in the spiritual and natural worlds simultaneously. Things that can be seen with our eyes are called natural, and things that cannot be seen with our eyes are called spiritual or invisible. Earthly things are called natural, and things in heaven are called spiritual. The spiritual realm is unlimited, while the natural realm is limited.

What we do in our day to day life depends on which realm we are more accustomed to operating in or by which we are guided. If we look into the natural realm, there is not much we can do and have. However, if we learn to live in the spirit, we have everything unlimited.

Are you discouraged or disappointed today? If you are, it will be because something has gone wrong in the natural realm, or something is not working as you wanted it to.

Worry comes as a result of caring only about the natural things while ignoring the spiritual. Things in the natural realm will disappoint us and make life meaningless, because we are created to live by our spirit, and not by our natural senses.

We are spirit beings, and we need to draw our resources from the spirit world in order to accomplish our mission on the earth. The reason most believers achieve so little in their lives, is because they know only how to live based on what is available to them in the natural realm.

We see the things in the natural realm with our physical eyes, while we can see the things in the spirit realm with our spiritual eyes or eyes of our heart. We respond to the things in the natural realm with our five senses, while we respond to the things in the spirit realm with our sixth sense, called faith. Faith is a quality of our spirit, not our mind or soul.

How do we tap into the invisible realm in order to receive these spiritual blessings?

Faith is the only substance that connects the natural and the spiritual realms and the visible and the invisible realms. Faith is the assurance of things not seen. "Things not seen" does not mean that they do not exist. They do exist, but they are invisible to the natural eyes.

The only language the supernatural or the invisible world responds to is faith-filled words. You have to see the invisible, and you need to talk it as if it was visible, and then you will have what you spoke out or confessed with your mouth.

A centurion came to Jesus and asked Him to heal his servant. Jesus replied and said to him that He would come and heal his servant. The centurion said to Jesus that it was not necessary for Him to come to his house, but to just speak the Word and his servant would be made whole.

Jesus was surprised by what he heard. He was surprised because He found a man who understood the principle of how to tap into the supernatural. Please know that all truths are parallel; thus, the centurion used his authority in the natural realm in order to illustrate what could be possible in the spiritual realm.

When we release a faith-filled word, it goes into the invisible realm and accomplishes what it is being sent for.

The worlds that we see were made by things that were not seen, which is the Word of God (Hebrews 11:3). God starts everything in the invisible realm, and He expects us to do the same.

We have His image and likeness, and we are supposed to act like Him. We can only call into the natural realm those things that already exist and can seen in the supernatural realm.

We cannot create anything, for God alone is the only Creator. The difference between our faith and God's faith is that our faith calls things from the supernatural realm into the natural realm. God's faith calls things out of nothingness into existence (Romans 4:17).

God speaks to create things. We speak to manifest things. Everything that we need already exists in the supernatural realm. That is why the scripture says He has blessed us with all "spiritual" blessings. Our blessings are spiritual in nature, which have got the potential to manifest in the natural realm when we speak the right words.

One day Jesus and His disciples were in a town called Bethany. He was hungry and looked for something to eat. He saw a fig tree and found nothing on it to eat but leaves. He cursed the tree, and the tree was dried up from the roots. The disciples marveled at it, and He explained to them the secret behind the incident.

Mark 11:22-23 (KJV) says, "And Jesus answering saith unto them, Have faith in God. For verily I say unto you, That whosoever shall say unto this mountain, be thou removed, and be thou cast into the sea; and shall not doubt in his heart, but shall believe that those things which he saith shall come to pass; he shall have whatsoever he saith."

A mountain is made out of visible substances like rocks and soil, and it takes extraordinary power to move a mountain. Jesus said our words filled with faith have more power than any big mountain. The invisible has more power than the visible. Thus, the invisible realm is superior to the visible realm.

Genesis 1: 2 & 3 says, that the earth was without form and void, and darkness was upon the face of the earth. God looked at the darkness and said, "Let there be light." The light appeared in that split second. The light existed before He spoke the Word, and the word He spoke brought the light from the invisible realm to the visible realm. Every time He spoke the word, it brought the corresponding action into the visible realm.

The invisible realm is unlimited, while the visible realm is limited. Jesus took the five loaves and two fishes, gave thanks, and gave to the disciples to feed the five thousand. The bread and fish were multiplied to feed the five thousand that were present. If there were ten thousand people, the bread and fish would have multiplied accordingly.

God has made unlimited resources available to us. He has made unlimited power, wisdom, finances, wealth, etc. available to us. It is up to us how much we are willing to receive.

David told Goliath what he saw in the invisible realm about what he was going to do to him. We read in 1 Samuel 17: 46 (KJV) "This day the Lord will deliver thee into mine hand; and I will smite thee, and take thy head from thee; and I will give the carcasses of the host of the Philistines this day unto the fowls of the air, and to the wild beasts of the earth; that all the earth may know that there is a God in Israel." He had what he spoke. He was speaking words filled with faith, and he took action and saw the result he wanted.

We are not created to live according to our natural senses just because we are living in a visible realm. We are spiritual beings sent by God to accomplish a mission on this earth. God wants things to be done on this earth as he does it in heaven. He wants earth to be an extension of heaven and everything that is in heaven. He equipped us with a heavenly substance called faith to accomplish it.

The Bible says God has dealt to each one a measure of faith (Romans 12:3b). Faith is an invisible substance that connects between the visible and the invisible realms. Faith is not what you feel; faith is something you "have." Jesus didn't say if you "feel" little faith as of the mustard seed, but He said if you "have ..."

Faith is the opposite of feeling, just like doubt is the opposite of belief. Having is possessing, not feeling. You cannot possess your feelings. To have something means you have it in your possession. If I say I have five dollars in my pocket, that means if you check my pocket, you will find five dollars. If I say, I feel there is five dollars in my pocket, the five dollars may or may not be in my pocket. The people who do great exploits for God are those who see and live according to what they see in the invisible realm.

Our origin is not on earth or the nation where you were born. When you die, you don't go back to the place of your natural birth but to where your spirit was born. The Apostle Paul says, "Set your mind on things above, not on things on the earth" (Colossians 3:2). Things of the spirit are invisible to the natural eyes, but they are not "invisible" or nonexistent.

Invisible things are more real than the things in the natural realm. Visible things are only a reflection of things that are in the invisible realm. God never expects us to do anything for Him based on the natural. To the natural eyes or senses it may seem foolishness or impossible.

This is why many ignore the dreams and visions that God gives them. They would rather live a miserable and unfulfilled life. Your visions and dreams are spiritual in nature, and they need "stuff" from the spiritual realm to accomplish it on this earth. How do we obtain the spiritual stuff that we need to fulfill our dream? Is it available to anyone who needs it or only to those who are super spiritual?

The Bible is full of examples of those people who looked beyond the natural realm, followed the invisible realm, and achieved great things in their lives. They apprehended the supernatural realm while they lived in the natural realm. When God tells you to do something, He tells you based on what He sees in the spiritual realm. If you try to accomplish it based on what you have in the natural realm, disappointment will be the result.

A few in the Bible reached out into the supernatural realm and lived a life that is available to us now. Men like Enoch, Noah, Abraham, David and Elijah are some examples. Jesus said Abraham desired to see His days and saw it three thousand five hundred years before Christ was born (John 8:56).

God created everything we see on this earth from the invisible realm. Everything visible came out of the invisible realm. The Bible says in Hebrews 11: 3 "By faith we understand that the worlds were framed by the word of God, so that the things which are seen were not made of things which are visible."

This means this world existed in the invisible realm before it manifested in the natural realm. God didn't create the visible things with natural substances, but He created them with an invisible substance.

Before God spoke the word to create everything, these were hidden in the spiritual realm or in Him. When He spoke the Word, the invisible became visible. It was the faith contained in His Word that brought the invisible realm to the visible realm. God wants us to do the same because we are created in His own likeness and in His image.

When God called out Abraham, he didn't obey God based on what he saw in the natural realm. In the first call God specifically said, "....to a land that I am going to show you" (Genesis 12: 1b). If he had waited around to see something in the natural realm in order to start his journey, he would not have attained the testimony as the father of faith. But He saw the invisible realm that was hidden in God's Word, and he started his journey.

Abraham didn't see anything in the natural realm to believe. This doesn't mean what he believed didn't exist. He saw it with the eyes of his heart or spirit, and took action. The reason he was called the father of faith is not because he was the most holy person who ever lived or because he preached more sermons than any one of us.

On the contrary, Abraham never preached a sermon, and he made mistakes as any one of us has. He obtained that testimony because *he believed* the invisible realm more than the visible realm. He followed what he saw in the spirit regardless of circumstances that showed the opposite. He was the first one to attempt something of that nature in the Bible.

When God gave him the promises, there was nothing to show as evidence. In Moses' case God equipped him with miracles. But when Abraham explained his vision to his family there was nothing tangible but only "words." When the people heard him speak, he spoke like he saw something; he was not sharing a story or a dream. He shared with such a conviction that even his nephew wanted to go with him without knowing where they were going.

Abraham saw the invisible realm, and it was clearer to him than the natural things. Whatever God spoke, already existed in the spiritual realm. How can a man become a father of many nations when he doesn't have a child of his own? There were times Abraham doubted and lost sight of the spiritual realm, while looking at the natural realm.

That was when he made terrible mistakes. His wife Sarah couldn't see the invisible realm, and so she persuaded Abraham to act based on what she saw in the natural realm. When we try to do the spiritual based on what we see in the natural, we make the same kind of mistakes and end up with tremendous loss.

Anyone can do the impossible if he sees the invisible realm. Your nationality, your financial or educational background are not the determining factors; but rather, can you see something that others cannot see? This is why God always tells ordinary people to do extraordinary things.

Moses ran away from Egypt and chose to suffer with his brethren. You may ask why did Moses run away from Egypt, from being the prince of Pharaoh enjoying all the luxuries and respect that he had? The writer of Hebrews tells us the reason why he refused to be called the son of Pharaoh's daughter.

Hebrews 11:24-27 (KJV) says, "By faith Moses, when he came to years, refused to be called the son of Pharaoh's daughter; choosing rather to suffer affliction with the people of God, than to enjoy the pleasures of sin for a season ... By faith he forsook Egypt, not fearing the wrath of the king: for he endured, as seeing Him who is invisible."

Moses saw the invisible and found there was something better for him to do than be in the palace. He understood the reason for him being in the palace was temporary, preparing him for a greater purpose. He followed the invisible for the next forty years before he saw any natural manifestation.

The Bible says God has blessed us with all spiritual blessings in heavenly places (Ephesians 1:3). *Spiritual* means invisible. God already blessed you with all the blessings that you ever need, but they are not in the visible realm. That doesn't mean they don't exist, and they are not there. They were there before you were born because spiritual things are eternal, and natural things are temporal.

Then why are many not receiving it, you might ask? Because there are only a few who actually follow the spirit and the invisible realm, because it doesn't make natural sense to many; they follow the natural realm and miss the spiritual realm. Most miss the spiritual realm because they always want to be in control. You cannot control the spirit world, it controls you.

When people hear the word *spirit* or *spiritual*, many have a weird feeling because they think it is spooky or unreal. *Spiritual* simply means "invisible" to your natural eyes. For example, when God brought the people of Israel out of Egypt to take them to the Promised Land, he told them that He was taking them to a land that flowed with milk and honey.

They couldn't see the land with their natural eyes, but they could see it in their spirit based on what God said.

Why did He tell them so much about the land with their natural eyes, but they could see it in their spirit based on what God said?

Why did He tell them so much about the land and what was in it before they were even near it?

He wanted them to see it in the invisible realm and walk as if they saw it in the natural realm. He was painting a picture in their hearts of the land they were going to possess.

God wanted them to be guided by what they saw in the invisible realm rather than what they saw in the wilderness they were in. God knew if they couldn't possess it in their heart, they wouldn't possess it in the natural realm.

God uses natural things that are familiar to us to show us what is in the invisible realm. Too many times they lost sight of the spiritual realm and responded to life based on what they saw in the natural realm, and thus most did not receive their blessings. What the Israelites inherited, was a spiritual inheritance.

Principles of Faith

Principle #1: Before you possess something in the natural realm, you need to see and possess it in your spirit.

Although they didn't see the land of Canaan with their natural eyes, that didn't mean it didn't exist. The promise and the land existed before they were born.

Principle #2: You cannot see something that does not exist either in the natural or in the spiritual realms.

The number one principle of sight is that you cannot see something that doesn't exist. Whether it is with the natural eyes or the spiritual eyes. If you can see something, it is there somewhere. Some are in the visible realm, and others are in the invisible realm.

Principle #3: Everything visible comes out of the invisible realm.

God created the visible realm with the substance that is invisible to our natural eyes.

Principle #4: God starts everything first in the invisible realm.

We need to follow and imitate Him as His dear children. We need to learn to operate as God operates.

Principle #5: If you can imagine something in your mind, that means it already exists somewhere.

You cannot imagine something if it does not already exist. If you can see it in the spirit, it has the potential to manifest in the natural realm.

Principle #6: The invisible realm is the blueprint of the visible realm.

God wants to manifest on earth what is in heaven. This is why we pray for His will to be done on earth as it is in heaven.

Some people have difficulty believing in things that they cannot see with their natural eyes. The Bible calls them natural or carnal Christians (1 Corinthians 2:14). Carnal people only mind the things that are carnal or natural. If they cannot touch and feel, they won't believe, and so their world is limited to what they can see with their natural eyes.

I call them "Christian chickens" because they are always looking at things on earth and are thus going to be a prey to this world and its systems. The truth is everyone sees with their spirit all the time, whether they believe it or not.

What you imagine in your heart about your future is spiritual imagination. What you constantly imagine in your heart whether it is negative or positive has got power to manifest in the natural realm.

Others, when they hear the word "spirit" think that only a select few are able to see spiritual things. Actually, anyone who is alive, has the potential to see and receive from the spirit world because you are a spiritual being.

Another misconception people have when they hear the word *spirit*, is that all they can think about is heaven. When the Bible says to walk in the Spirit. It doesn't mean we have to walk in heaven or we have to wait to get to heaven to walk in the Spirit. It means to mind things that are spiritual and to think on those things that are eternal, and not temporal.

If we do this, we won't fulfill the lust of the flesh. the flesh always looks at the natural realm and responds based on what it sees. Many precious saints of God bury their dreams and potential because they think these are too insignificant to do anything with their natural lives. It is not because of their humility they say that, but because they are too "fleshy" and carnally-minded. They mind the things of the natural-man and thus limit their spirit-man.

They always see a lion outside, and have such an excuse, because their flesh is too strong for their spirit. What makes a spirit *a spirit* is that it is not limited by time or space. Your spirit is unlimited, and you can achieve unlimited things in this life. Time or space does not limit you. We are eternal, and what makes a thing eternal is that it is always in existence.

With the fall of Adam, our spirit became separated from God, and thus we lost the ability to be controlled by our spirit. Instead, the soul[1] took charge of our life, and we became a limited being controlled by our five natural senses.

At the time of our born-again experience, however, our spirit obtained life from God, and our spirit was "born" a second time. When a person is born again at any age, he still has a mind that is much older than his born-again spirit.

Just like a big brother likes to bully and be in charge of the younger ones, our soul will still try to keep our spirit and body under its control. However, the soul is limited, while the spirit is unlimited. Our soul has only limited power to comprehend ideas and concepts; this is why many cannot accept God in their minds.

Our spirit-man needs to be trained and equipped by the Word of God to exercise authority. This is why the Bible says of John the Baptist in Luke 1:80, "So the child grew and became strong in spirit …" This means His spirit was much stronger than His soul or body.

Our body is our neutral part, and as such it will always follow either our soul or our spirit. Our body is lifeless without our soul

---

1 Mind, emotions, and will

and spirit. Some think their body is their problem. The real problem is our unrenewed carnal mind.

Thus, your body is not the problem. Rather, the real problem is your carnal mind. Your body is a blessing if you take care of it according to godly principles. But if you use your body to do things that are contrary to God's Word, you will reap corruption in this life.

It is sad to say that many born again Christians cannot think beyond their bodies. They don't look at their bodies as the means to accomplish spiritual things on this earth. They think that their bodies and the pleasure these bring is all they have. Oh, what a tormenting life that would be to be mindful only of the things of the body!

The Apostle Paul was not guided by the things he saw with his natural eyes. His testimony was "I was not disobedient to the heavenly vision" (Acts 26:19). He was guided by the invisible realm.

He rejoiced and enjoyed his life in the natural realm though it was not pleasant outwardly. If anyone should have worried and complained, that should have been Apostle Paul. But rather, he wrote to the people who were "worried" about him being in prison, to rejoice instead.

When he was persecuted, he considered it as a joy for the sake of Christ. The reason was that his body was brought under such submission to his spirit, that he could go through any turmoil and come out victoriously. He said, "Follow[2] me as I follow Christ" (1 Corinthians 11:1 KJV).

What he was saying, was to follow him as he followed his spirit. It was not a call to do everything exactly as he did. If so, we will

---

2 Imitate (Greek)

miss our own calling. Some do take it that way, and teach others not to marry because he was not married. No one can literally do everything as he did. We have to follow with our spirit the things that are invisible and thereby fulfill the purpose and the call that God has placed on our own lives.

Are you worried about how you are going to have the things in order to fulfill your dream?

Do not look into the natural or visible realm. Rather, look into the invisible realm, at the unlimited resources and blessings that you can have more of than you can ever have in the natural realm.

How do we tap into the invisible realm in order to receive our spiritual blessings?

Faith is the only substance that connects between the natural and the supernatural world. Faith is the assurance of things not seen. Words that we speak by faith are the only medium by which we receive from the invisible realm. Words filled with faith attract God, while negative words attract the demonic forces.

You may ask, "Why are things not happening when we speak?"

Jesus said if we abide in Him, and His Words abides in us, whatever we ask we shall receive (John 15 :7) What God has made available to us is unlimited resources, unlimited wisdom, unlimited finances, unlimited power; but it is up to us how much we are willing to receive.

The secret lies in the words that the centurion spoke to Jesus. Matthew 8:8 (KJV) says, "The centurion answered and said, 'Lord, I am not worthy that thou shouldest come under my roof: but speak the word only, and my servant shall be healed.'"

When we are filled to the brim with the Word of God and speak only the Word, we shall begin to see mighty miracles in our lives.

If God has chosen us before the foundation of the earth, we must be existing somewhere in this universe. Our life didn't begin when we were born on this earth. We are a spiritual being living in eternity, and brought to this earth to accomplish something for God.

Jesus taught us to pray the same thing, "Let your kingdom come and your will be done on this earth as it is in heaven."

This means He wants the invisible things to be revealed on earth as it is in heaven. He wants the spiritual realm to be manifested in the natural realm.

The Bible says God's will concerning our lives is good, acceptable and perfect (Romans 12:2). "Spiritual blessings" means that whatever you receive from the invisible or God is a spiritual blessing.

When the people of Israel reached the wilderness, they ran out of water. They complained and murmured based on what they saw in the natural realm.

God was not worried about the situation. In the invisible realm the water they needed already existed. God told Moses to command the rock to bring forth water, and when he commanded, the water came out rushing out and flowed like a river (Psalm 105:41).

Where was that water coming from? Or where was the water before it manifested in the natural realm? To the natural eyes it is impossible to figure out water in a desert place. The water was called a "spiritual drink" in 2 Corinthians 10:3.

They needed food in the wilderness, and it looked impossible in the natural realm to feed at least four million people in a desert. The invisible realm was capable of not only feeding four million, as it still feeds almost six billion people a day. God sent the bread from heaven called "manna," and fed them in the wilderness for forty years. The Bible calls it a "spiritual meat" in 2 Corinthians 10:3.

Whenever I ask people to name some of the spiritual blessings that they know, they answer me saying, "Peace, joy, tongues, love, etc." They can't think that everything they see came out of the invisible realm.

The food that we eat and the water we drink were created by God; as all created things came out of things that are not visible (Hebrews 11:3). Everything in the natural realm came out of the spiritual realm. Without the spiritual realm there is no natural realm.

So, when the Bible talks about the spiritual blessings, it is talking about what is in the unseen realm, and not merely spiritual gifts. If you receive something from God, it is a spiritual blessing.

Whether it is cup of water or a pair of shoes, a car or a house; if it is a gift from God, it is spiritual. Many are waiting to go to heaven, but do not have a clue of what it is really like in heaven.

The Bible mentions many things that are in heaven. There is water, bread, buildings, gold and precious metals and stones, roads, trees, animals, angels, fruits, rivers, music and musical instruments, crowns and thrones. For almost everything you see on earth, the original is in heaven or in the spiritual realm.

When the Bible talks about spiritual blessings, it is not talking about intangible or unrealistic things. It is in fact talking about things that do exist, in the invisible realm. The Bible is a spiritual book, and words written in it are spiritual. Jesus said, "The words that I speak to you are spirit, and they are life" (John 6:63).

Whatever you need to fulfill your dream or vision already exists in the invisible realm. It is up to you to receive it or ignore it.

When Jesus fed the five thousand in the wilderness where did that bread and fish came from?

You may say Jesus did a miracle. Jesus unlocked the invisible realm with the visible realm, and thus the bread and fish were multiplied in thousands. They were already there in the invisible realm, but the miracle made it visible.

Principle # 7: Whatever you need from the supernatural realm, you need to initiate in the natural realm under God's guidance.

Every action on earth will have an opposite or corresponding reaction from heaven. A miracle is something you initiate in the natural realm according to supernatural guidance. No miracle ever happened until someone initiated it on the earth. When the people of Israel reached the Red Sea, they cried out to God for help.

God told Moses, "Why are you crying to me, stretch your hand over the sea and divide it" (Exodus 14:15-16). The widow in Elijah's time gave him bread to eat from the little she had, and thereby she received a miracle. Another widow in Elisha's time came to him for help and asked him for a miracle. He told her to go and pour out the oil she had into empty jars. She did it, and she received her miracle.

The woman with the issue of blood pressed through the crowd and touched the hem of Jesus' garments, and thus she received her healing.

What if she had just sat at her home, and prayed to God to send a miracle?

Are you waiting for your miracle for years, and it is not coming your way?

A miracle is passing you by, everyday; and if you don't receive it, someone next to you in line will get it.

As someone said, "If you want to walk on the water you need to get out of the boat."

Name and receive your God-ordained spiritual blessings today.

Salvation is a spiritual blessing. God has paid a high price for the salvation of the entire human race. It is His desire that not even a little one should perish. Matthew 18:14 says, "Even so it is not the will of your Father who is in heaven that one of these little ones should perish."

We don't need to allow the Pharaoh to hold back anyone for when God has paid the price for their redemption. We need to fight until we see the total victory.

7 KINDS OF BELIEVERS

Fourth Kind
Only Wives Are Saved

This is very common in Indian churches. I have seen hundreds of wives come to the Lord and serve Him in churches, but their husbands remain in Egypt and sometimes their children also follow their father; although other times, they follow their mother. Any meetings you attend there will be more women than men.

Many times, I have seen the husbands are alcoholics. I believe that alcoholism is a spirit of Egypt, because it never lets them use their mind for anything good.

As long as we remain in Egypt, we cannot understand God's purpose for our lives. There is always conflict in these homes because the wife knows the plan of God and what needs to be done. When she shares that with her husband, it doesn't make sense to him, so he will pick a fight, and so most of the time there won't be peace in the family.

They will never reach financial freedom, because the husband makes money and spends almost all the money on drinking with his friends, Lord, please have mercy upon such families.

Again, dear ones, don't give up your fight. As the Bible says, "And let us not grow weary while doing good, for in due season we shall reap if we do not lose heart" (Galatians 6:9).

Once we understand that it is God's desire that none should perish, we can have confidence that we are going to have the ultimate victory over the devil. We don't have to let anyone go to eternity without Christ.

In the cases above, the best thing the wives should do is to continue their faith with pure hearts and genuine love for their husbands and children.

For we know that our fight is not with flesh and blood but with evil forces that blind people from seeing the light. The devil is the father of lies, and he only speaks lies. He is an expert at making people believe a lie and convincing them that what they believe is the truth.

Thus, many have a distorted view of spiritual warfare. Please know that the devil will always act up according to what you believe he can do. He can act "like" a roaring lion, but he is not a lion. He puts on a show. He can also act like an angel of light.

If we need to see our loved ones come to the Lord, we need to really look into what hinders them from coming to Him.

Some of you may admire certain individuals for what they say and do about spiritual warfare. Let me tell you; our Lord Jesus is my favorite person from whom I learn victorious spiritual warfare. I like to face the devil as Jesus encountered him. The Bible says, "... As He is, so are we in this world" (1 John 4 :17b).

CHAPTER SIX

Understanding Spiritual Warfare

In the book of Genesis, when God created Adam and put him in the garden, we don't see God warning His son about the devil. My question is, "Why didn't God tell or warn Adam and Eve about the devil or the serpent?"

I have read the early chapters of Genesis many times over, and I couldn't find a scripture where God warned His son, Adam, about an enemy. If the devil was that powerful and was waiting to get His son, Adam was in trouble. Why didn't an all-knowing Father even mention that ugly devil?

I would not leave my children in the face of danger when they cannot help themselves. I would be a foolish father to do such a thing. I will not leave one of my kids in the city of Bombay and expect him or her to find their way. If I love my children that much and care for them, how much more our Heavenly Father loves you and me and cares for us.

Some of you may think that God knew it all from the beginning and so He just left them there to see His plans accomplished. No, dear child of God, it was not His original intent to let His Son die for our sins.

Are you willing to let your only child go to a mission field and never see them again? I don't think so. God gave me an answer that will startle your theology; so, hold on to your seat!

God didn't think it was important to discuss the devil with his son, Adam. The devil was not a threat to God and His purpose, as some of us might think these days.

God equipped His son with the most powerful weapon possible. He gave him His Word. As long as they kept and obeyed that Word, no enemy was powerful enough to do them any harm.

As long as Adam and Eve obeyed God's commandment; the devil couldn't even peek into the garden. Do you see what I see, dear saints of God?

How stupid some Christians act before the ugly devil, thinking it is their responsibility to defeat him! With all the nonsense about spiritual warfare going around today, people have no time to read and meditate on the Word.

They have money and time to go and hear any limp theology about the devil, but no time for God. They have time to talk about and blame the devil for anything that goes wrong with their lives, work, church or nation. They will never take time to look into their individual responsibilities to keep and obey the Word of God.

Because God gave his son, Adam, this powerful spiritual weapon; and the enemy knew that he couldn't come to Adam for a face-to-face battle; if he had done that, he would have lost the war, because God gave the dominion of the earth only to Adam. God gave the title deed or lease agreement to Adam. He didn't entrust anything to the devil.

The devil was an illegal intruder in the garden. So, the devil had to find a different means to get those people to listen him. The devil knew the only way he could get his evil purpose accomplished in man was to make him first disobey God's Word.

Sin, curse, death, poverty, pride, sickness, murder, adultery, fornication, idolatry and every other evil that you can imagine was in the devil, waiting for an opportunity to get into human lives.

Dear saints of God, the devil didn't have any other way; and he cannot invent a new way, other than to make you and I transgress God's Word. He deceived them, and the moment they transgressed God's Word, sin entered man and the world; and man became spiritually dead.

Then sin, sickness, curses, death and all evil were given an entrance to operate on the face of the earth. If Adam would have kept the Word of God, no devil was powerful enough to come near them.

Man had more authority and power than the devil in his original position. God has not changed His original purpose concerning us. Throughout the Bible, He tells His children to keep His Word, and they will be the most powerful forces on earth.

Now the question is, which *word* of God is a child of God supposed to keep?

We live in the New Covenant. We should not mix the New with the Old Covenant. Many people do that, and thus they bring upon themselves unnecessary troubles and curses. If we go back to the Old Covenant then we are required to keep the entire law, which no one did, or could ever. Many believers pick and choose what they like from the Old Covenant to add to their religiosity.

The only place the Word "warfare" is mentioned in the New Testament is in 2 Corinthians 10:4 saying, "For the weapons of our warfare are not carnal, but mighty through God to the pulling down of strongholds."

The next verse explains the purpose of those weapons, and where to use them. The first purpose of these weapons is to cast down imaginations. Our war is against imaginations. Our warfare is information warfare.

Where does the imagination exist? It exists in the minds of people. In the natural realm, during wars between countries, the main weapons are not guns and bombs. There are also media weapons.

The news plays an important role about who is going to win the war. Even if you have the best technology and weapons, without the right information, and making your enemy believe the wrong information, weapons alone don't necessarily ensure a victory.

The Apostle Paul explains in the next verse clearly what those strongholds are, and where they exist. Hence, 2 Corinthians 10:5 says, "Casting down arguments and every high thing that exalts itself against the knowledge of God, bringing every thought into capacity to the obedience of Christ."

A stronghold does not exist in the skies, but in the minds of people. He is talking here about imaginations and knowledge and bringing these to the obedience of Christ.

Mostly, we don't fight against demons with horns and hooves like the ones we see in Hollywood movie productions. In fact, the devil never appeared to anyone like that in the Bible. He always came with ideas and opinions, creating an imagination in the minds of people against the principle of God. Every cult, religion, and "ism" is a demon-inspired idea and diabolic information.

We are constantly at war with information and knowledge that are contrary to God's knowledge. The number one weapon that the devil uses today to keep many precious people in bondage, is the media.

What is media? It is often information and pictures that fight against the truth and order of God's Word. You may say, I am tempted to do things that are contrary to God's Word. What is temptation? It is thoughts or desires; and the bottom line is that they are information. If you can win the war against information in your mind, you are ready to do some exploits for God.

The mind is bombarded with thoughts and imaginations every second, while we are awake and while we sleep. We need to know how to keep our thoughts and minds captivated, obedient to Christ and His Word. It takes discipline to live a life that is victorious.

The devil came to tempt Jesus after He had fasted for forty days. He came with information or knowledge that was contrary to God's Word; and thus, Jesus *educated* the devil with the right information. Every reply of Jesus was from the Word of God. He didn't make things up; He just spoke the very words that were written by brother Moses.

That is all it takes to defeat any ugly devil that is trying to get you into trouble. One single word in the Bible has got more power than Satan and his entire dark forces combined.

No one has ever tasted even the least of the power of God's Word. His power is in His Word. Every power, energy, and force that is in the universe is from God. Whether it is atomic, chemical, heat, or electric, the origin of all power is God.

The Bible says, "... Power belongs to God." (Psalm 62:11).

Do you see something powerful? He didn't yell or scream at the devil. He just had a communication, and the power of the communication was that He spoke the truth.

Can we do this, dear saints of God? Can we stop living stupid before the world and the devil?

Based on the above scripture our warfare is not against principalities and Satan, but against imaginations and knowledge that are contrary to God's knowledge; first in our mind, then in our neighbors' minds, and then in the minds of nations.

I am believing in the Lord to write a book called, *Spiritual Warfare According to Jesus*. How did He face demons and transform fishermen into mighty Apostles?

When Jesus came to do His earthly ministry, He didn't start with cussing at principalities. Rather, He did something very powerful. He knew more than all of us know about how to fight the enemy. When He started His ministry, the religious Jews were following the Old Testament, but had no clue about what they were doing.

Outside Israel, the world was following the Buddha and Hindu philosophies.

Because Jesus was a smart guy who knew everything, He knew exactly what needed to be done in order to turn the people to God. The first word that came out of His mouth was not "Hey guys get rid of those demons off of your lives so that you can enter the kingdom of God." Instead He said in Matthew 4:17, "… Repent; for the kingdom of God is at hand."

Repent means to change your mind. Change your mind, means to get rid of the information that is in your mind; because that is what is making you do what you are doing now.

Fill your mind with new information or knowledge that is according to God, and you will be ready to enter the Kingdom. His warfare was to pull down strongholds from the minds of people and His disciples; He did that through teaching them the principles of the Kingdom of God.

If you read the Sermon on the Mount and compare it with the mindset of the people of His day, everything He said was just the opposite of what they had believed for hundreds of years. Some went crazy after hearing His teaching, and some accepted it and changed their minds.

Every Word that came out of the mouth of Jesus was poking the mindset of the people. His war was with the information that the devil had packed into the minds of the people. He attacked it with the Word of God.

He told us to do the same. Just before the ascension, He told His disciples to do the same. In Matthew 28:19 (KJV) says, "Go ye therefore, and teach all nations, baptizing them in the name of the Father, and of the Son, and of the Holy Spirit."

Every feeling that you have, whether joy, crying, laughing, love, or attraction to someone—all happens because your brain receives information from the nervous system or body parts, and makes your body react to that information.

The entire world functions based on information they receive. The universe and solar system work according to information; that is, the Word of God. They have been programmed by the Word of God when God created them.

The most popular computer word-processing program is also called "Word[3]."

Psalm 19:2 & 3 (KJV) says, "Day unto day uttereth speech, and night unto night sheweth knowledge. There is no speech nor language, where their voice is not heard."

---

3 ® Microsoft Word

The other scripture that we usually quote regarding spiritual battles, is Ephesians 6:12, "For we wrestle not against flesh and blood, but against principalities..." Here, the word "wrestle" is used instead of "war." There is a big difference between wrestling and war.

We can war with our enemy face to face or from thousands of miles away. Most of us have watched wrestling on television so you know what Paul used as an illustration.

Paul knew exactly what he was talking about. In his time, one of the main sports of the Romans was wrestling; wrestling between both humans and animals.

Wrestling is something that happens in close proximity. I cannot wrestle with some forces in outer space. We are wrestling with principalities to keep away information and knowledge that they send to keep us defeated and ineffective for God.

If you study any spiritual battle in the Bible, or in your life, you will come to the conclusion that they all began with some kind of imagination or thoughts. If you look back in your life and examine the times you were defeated in your life, those were all because you believed in some wrong information, or you didn't have the right information. We are guided and governed by our thoughts. Our thoughts are like the rudder of a ship.

If we desire to win anyone to Christ, we need to use the principles or warfare that are set forth in the New Testament.

We don't fight against Pharaoh as Moses did in Egypt. We are dealing with spiritual strongholds made out of wrong information in the minds of people. Let us fight with wisdom, and win every battle the devil has formed against us.

7 KINDS OF BELIEVERS

Fifth Kind
Saved, but Material Blessings Remain in Egypt

After the ninth plague, Pharaoh called Moses and said all the people can go and worship the Lord but their flocks and herds should remain in Egypt. Exodus 10:24 (KJV) says, "And Pharaoh called unto Moses, and said, "Go ye, serve the LORD; only let your flocks and your herds be kept back. Let your little ones also go with you."

Wow! Dear child of God, have you seen someone who is saved and not blessed materially? I have seen hundreds and hundreds of genuine believers who are saved, but struggling to survive. Every day is a struggle to move forward not having enough to provide for the family.

It is the devil's plan to keep us financially bound so that we will not fulfill our destiny, and we won't be able to help the church to get the job done.

In the Old Testament times, flocks and herds were the wealth of the people. You knew a person's wealth by knowing how many cattle they had. We read about Job that he was a wealthy man. He had seven thousand sheep, three thousand camels, five hundred yokes of oxen, five hundred she asses, and a very great household, so that this man was the greatest of all the people of the east (Job 1:3).

I believe the biggest deception that the devil has played on believers world-wide, is to make them believe that the wealth of this world is only for the ungodly. The devil has made them believe that if you are a child of God you are not supposed to have much wealth. They use scriptures like Hebrews 11:13-16 where it speaks of those who lived like pilgrims and looked for a city whose foundation was laid by God. They use Abraham as an example of leaving his father's house to inherit eternal blessing.

However, the Bible says in Genesis 13:2 that Abraham was wealthy and had silver, gold, servants, and cattle: "And Abram was very rich in cattle, in silver, and in gold." Was he saved? Could he receive the call of God as no one has ever received it, and have silver and gold?

The Bible says that if we are the children of God, we inherit the faith of Abraham. What is the faith of Abraham?

Is it to remain poor, wretched and stingy? Then the world looks at us and says, here is a group of people who always want something for nothing. The faith of Abraham was to call those things when they do not exist, into the visible realm as if they really exist (Romans 14:7).

God's desire was not to leave even a hoof in Egypt. Moses said in Exodus 10:26, "Our cattle also shall go with us; there shall not a hoof be left behind ..." This means we can't even leave a can of soda behind, when we depart from Egypt. Did you leave any of your "hooves" behind when you got saved?

I believe that according to God's point of view, salvation is for our entire being. The Bible never teaches a "spirit only salvation." In 3 John 2, we read that we should prosper in everything as our soul prospers. The Bible says in Proverbs 13:22 that the wealth of the wicked is laid up for the righteous.

I have had to reprogram the theology in my mind from what I'd learnt from my religious leaders. If had believed them, I would not have even started to fulfill the call God has for my life. Thank God for His mercy that endures forever.

Dear child of God, please don't accept your financial struggles as if these are from God. Keep the good fight to faith. I have seen in my life, the more I command the devil to loose my finances, the more I receive in order to do God's work.

It is God's desire to see His will be done on earth as it is in heaven. Imagine what would happen if the whole church grasped this and ran with it. Many have given themselves to be consumed by the enemy; as they have agreed with what the devil had offered them.

We can't say we are saved if half of what belongs to us still remains in Egypt. We don't need to accept the offer the enemy has put on our table. Please don't compromise with the enemy, thinking that at least all our household is saved; and so, why bother the devil again.

We should not stop until we receive everything that God has prepared for us. We are created to live in God's kingdom and enjoy its blessings.

Once we understand what God requires from us to enter and live in His kingdom, we need to fulfill those requirements in order to become citizens of his kingdom.

CHAPTER SEVEN

Be Born Again

One day, as teacher of the Pharisees, Nicodemus came to Jesus by night, appreciating Him for His works. Jesus turned and said to him something so powerful that it astounded Nicodemus.

I didn't understand the meaning of it either until last year, although I have been a Christian more than fifteen years. Jesus said, unless a man is born again, he cannot see the kingdom of God.

Why do we need to be born again? What does Jesus mean by born again? If we have to be born again, we were born once before.

John 3:3 & 5 says, "Jesus answered and said to him, "Most assuredly, I say to you, unless one is born again, he cannot see the kingdom of God." In verse five, "Jesus answered, 'Most assuredly, I say to you, unless one is born of water and the spirit, he cannot enter the kingdom of God.'"

When God created His son, Adam, according to Genesis chapter two, He formed man out of the dust. There was no life in that form until God breathed the breath of life into it. When God breathed His Spirit, man was born for the first time. Without God's Spirit the body is lifeless. We are not just a body, but we are a spirit-being.

Imagine how much time and money we spend to take care of the dust, our body, which is going to turn to dust again. Whatever is of the dust needs to go back to the dust. The more we try to deify the body the more problems it creates, and the more its demands increase.

God put Adam in the Garden of Eden and said to him to eat of all the trees of the garden, except the one in the midst of the garden, which was the tree of knowledge of good and evil.

God created man with a free will because He wanted His son to love Him by choice, not by obligation or compulsion; this is why He put that tree in the garden. He said, the day man eats from the tree of good and evil he shall surely die.

Before the fall, Adam had a perfect life. There was no sin, sickness, curse, poverty, sorrow, pain, strife or any other evil thing in the garden. Everything was perfect and luxurious; until Adam disobeyed God and ate the fruit of the tree, and he died.

It was a two-fold death. He died spiritually, and he lost his relationship with God. With that he lost all the blessings God had given him. It was a physical death, and he didn't live more than a day according to God, because a thousand years is as a day for Him. Adam lived only (930) years. It was a spiritual death; man was separated from God and was cast out of the garden.

The diagram below shows the before and after effects of mankind's fall:

Before the Fall	After the Fall
Healthy	Sick
Rich	Poor
Fruitful	Under a Curse
One with God	Barren
Son of God	Separated from God
Had Dominion	Bondage of the devil
Wise	Foolish
Holy	Unholy
Victorious	Defeated
Peaceful	Carnal
Spiritual	Sorrowful
In the Kingdom of God	In the kingdom of Darkness

Can you picture yourself living a life according to the blessings God had given us before the fall?

That was the original plan God had for you and me. Nowhere in the Bible do we read that He had changed His mind concerning us. God wants us to have good things in life.

The thief comes to steal, kill, and destroy. The Bible says, "No good thing will He withhold from those who walk uprightly" (Psalm 84:11b).

Adam didn't lack anything in the garden. He had the image and likeness of God in him. No one and nothing could defeat him. He was filled with God's glory. When he disobeyed God's Word, he lost every good thing.

Because of the fall, we had a total turn around in our nature. Every good thing was replaced by evil. Our character, nature, and mind were corrupted by sin. The diagram below shows the carnal nature each of us possesses.

The Carnal Nature

Mark 7:20-23	Galatians 5:17-23
Evil Thoughts	Adultery
Adulteries	Fornication
Fornication	Uncleanness
Murders	Lasciviousness
Thefts	Idolatry
Covetousness	Witchcraft
Wickedness	Hatred
Deceit	Variance
Lasciviousness	Emulations
Evil eye	Wrath
Blasphemy	Strife
Pride	Seditions
Foolishness	Heresies
	Envying
	Murders
	Drunkenness
	Reveling

The diagram above shows the nature human beings have before they come to Christ. The Bible says that such traits originate in mankind, and not in the devil. The church has been blaming the devil for all evil, when it really originates in the heart of man.

When a person initiates it, the devil takes advantage of it. The devil cannot do anything to us unless we initiate it. He can only stimulate, stipulate, and tempt us. Every person born under the sun after the similitude of Adam inherited the above due to our natural birth, and that is our first birth. The Bible clearly tells us that those who practice any of the above shall not inherit the kingdom of God.

Jesus is telling us to be born a second time. He is offering us an opportunity to get rid of all these evils. For us to enter His kingdom, we have to be born again—not after the similitude of the first Adam, but after the nature and likeness of the Last Adam, Jesus Christ.

Being born again is not a confession; it is a rebirth. Every time a child is born, there is pain involved. In the same way, we have to come out of the old into new life, and it is not an easy task. Just like a caterpillar comes out of the cocoon, there has to be a change and transformation in our lives after the born-again experience

Many limit their born-again experience to a confession, and thereafter live a miserable life for many years. They can't produce any fruit, and they become "pew potatoes" in the church building. They will be there week after week to attend the church meetings; and every time they open their mouths, they want to talk about the second coming of Christ or how terrible the devil is. They look to the second coming as an escape from this life on earth because they are fed up with their lives.

Dear Saints of God, please don't be faint-hearted. Open your eyes, and see the life God wants you and me to live. It is a God-kind of Life. He wants us to have everything we lost in the original fall. The purpose of redemption is restoration.

What did Jesus redeem us from? What did He restore? If He saved us from our sins, then everything we lost because of sin, must be restored. Since we lost our material blessings when we died spiritually; so, when we are spiritually alive, everything must be restored.

For us to receive everything back, Jesus is asking us to be born again. This is the only remedy for our dilemma.

If Adam had everything in the garden, we must become like Adam was originally, in order to have everything he had. We have to have the nature he had before the fall. We cannot become like Adam by our natural birth because the nature we inherited from Adam is corrupted by sin. So, we must be born after someone who has the nature of Adam before the fall.

God sent His son, born of a woman, in the likeness of a man. Jesus was born without sin, just like Adam was born in the beginning. Adam was born by the breath of God. Jesus was born by the breath of the Holy Spirit of God. Now, we must be born by Jesus Christ just like we are born from Adam.

The one is natural, and the other is spiritual. One is by flesh and blood; while the other is by water and Spirit. One is by human will, naturally; the other is by the will of God, by faith.

The Bible says in John 1:12, "Whoever believes in His name He has given us the authority to become a child of God." Just like we inherited our human nature from Adam through our natural birth, we inherit our spiritual nature from Jesus Christ by the born-again process. This is done through faith, by believing the Word of God.

The born-again experience is an exchange of natures. We trade our Adamic nature and inherit our original likeness and our image from the Last Adam, Jesus Christ. Romans 8:29 says, "For whom he did foreknew, he also predestined to be conformed to the image of his son, that he might be the Firstborn among many brethren."

Once we are born again, we have to educate our minds to think and act like a child of God. This doesn't happen automatically; it is a constant struggle and an intentional daily walk. This process is called renewing our mind by practicing the Word of God in our daily lives, which does the job for us.

Now we are going to look at the difference between the *first* Adam and the *last* Adam:

First Adam	**Last Adam**
Sinful	Sinless. He became sin for us
Sick	Healed all and bore our sickness
Poor	Rich, but became poor for us
Cursed	Blessed. He became a curse for us
Sorrowful	Full of joy, because He became a son of sorrows
Spiritually Died	Spiritually alive
Unholy	Holy
Disobedient	Obedient till death
Carnal	Spiritual
Enmity to God	Father was well-pleased. He became a Quickening Spirit

Born again means to start all over again. To start afresh, the first requirement is to put an end to the old man. If we don't put an end to the old man, we won't recognize the difference.

Born again, does not mean going to church services every Sunday.

Are you ready to stop where you are going, and start all over again?

Born again means to exchange your old nature for the new nature in Christ Jesus. This is a total change, and an absolute necessity in order to enter the Kingdom of God.

God is Holy, and no unholy being will even enter His kingdom. Revelation 21:8 says, "But the cowardly, unbelieving, abominable, murderers, sexually immoral ..." shall not inherit the kingdom of God. 1 Peter 1:16 says, "Be holy, for I am holy."

When we decide to be born again, we are making an agreement with God that we are willing to give up the old in order to receive the new. If this doesn't happen, all our singing and shouting is for vain.

The question is, can such a change be possible while we are living in this body? Can we become like Christ?

In the Old Testament, a couple of people got radically transformed; even their bodies were changed into something new.

Enoch was the first one. The Bible says he walked with God, and he was not. This means he walked with God to the extent that he became nothing; God become everything, and he was translated.

The next one was Moses. At the age of 120, he looked only 40 years old. When he came down from the mountain, his skin shone from the glory of God, and the people were afraid to look at him. His health and vigor didn't diminish by age. His eyesight didn't dim, and his stamina was as if he were forty years old. God Himself had to do a special funeral for him.

The third one was Elijah. He was taken up alive to heaven by fiery chariots. He had to be transformed before he was taken up; as no human being in their old nature, will even enter heaven. I believe if the Old Testament saints were transformed to the image and likeness of God under the old covenant, we can be transformed under the new covenant; only much more so.

The Bible says the glory of the ministry of the Spirit is much more glorious than the old covenant (2 Corinthians 3:7-8). My prayer is that all of us will be transformed into the image and likeness of God on this earth.

All creation is waiting for the manifestation of the sons of God (Romans 8 :21-22). Let us strive to become everything that God created us to be.

The Bible says in Romans 5:18, that by one man's disobedience, all were made sinners. In the same manner, by one man's obedience, we all become righteous.

If you and I need to know how we are supposed to function on this earth, we have to look at either Adam in Eden or Jesus Christ in the New Testament. They are the prototypes for our lives on this earth.

When Jesus said for us to be born again, He meant us to allow Him to change us to become what God has created us to be. This is why the Bible says in 2 Corinthians 5:17 (KJV) "If any man is in Christ he is a new creation; old things are passed away and behold everything becomes new."

As I was sharing this truth with someone, he asked me, "Doesn't the Bible say that if we believe in our heart that Jesus died and confess with our mouth, we shall be saved?" Another place in the Bible says, "All those who call upon the name of Lord shall be saved."

How far do you want to be saved? Do you just want to make it to heaven like the thief on the cross? He called upon the name of the Lord and was saved at the last minute.

Do you want to perish in the wilderness with your unfulfilled dreams? I don't want to live a life like that.

Do you want to live a life that is pleasing to the Lord, and be a blessing to thousands? I want to fulfill the promise of Abraham that God gave me through Christ (Galatians 3:14 & 29).

If you want to live a heaven-kind of life on earth, you need to change into a spiritual being. It is possible to live the life of heaven on this earth. Jesus taught us to pray for his Kingdom to come on this earth, and His will to be done on earth as it is in heaven.

Born again means we are dying to the old nature and saying yes to the new nature of our spirit. The old life is led by the flesh and mind. The new life is led by the spirit. The old life is earthward, while the new life is heavenward. The old life has the earthly nature, while the new life has the heavenly nature. The old nature causes us to have lack and poverty, while new nature enables us to experience the abundant life in Christ. As the Bible says, "The Lord is my shepherd I shall not lack" (Psalm 23:1).

7 KINDS OF BELIEVERS

Sixth Kind
Saved but Stuck in the Wilderness

Finally, at the tenth plague, Pharaoh let the people of Israel leave Egypt. Thus, it is interesting to read what he said to Moses. Exodus 12:31 & 32 (KJV) says, "And he called for Moses and Aaron by night, and said, 'Rise up, and get you forth from among my people, both ye and the children of Israel; and go, serve the LORD, as ye have said. Also take your flocks and your herds, as ye have said, and be gone, and bless me also.'"

This is the kind of deliverance we need to receive. God wants our entire household to be saved. God does not offer partial salvation. He is the God of abundance and wholeness. Jesus said that he had come to give us life, and life more abundantly (John 10:10).

Exodus 12:35 & 36 (KJV) says, "And the children of Israel did according to the word of Moses; and they borrowed of the Egyptians jewels of silver, and jewels of gold, and raiment. And the LORD gave the people favor in the sight of the Egyptians."

Many have limited themselves, and thereby fatally accepted what they have. They don't have a desire to get blessed. They think if God wants to bless them, He will drop it from heaven because He is God. Others believe it is a sin to ask God to bless us materially, because He might get angry. Others say you don't need to fight with the enemy to receive anything. So, if you were limping when you came to Christ, you need to keep limping until you get to heaven. If you were poor when you came to Christ, you need to remain poor, because He was poor.

There is a problem with this group. They are wonderfully and gloriously saved, but they are wandering in the wilderness. They are satisfied with what they have received, but cannot move into the destiny God has for them, because they cannot overcome their flesh.

Imagine if Moses had accepted what the Pharaoh had offered him first.

The Bible says God delights in the prosperity of His children (Psalm 35:27). Once you are in Christ, you are complete. I have explained this in detail in my other two books. Please see the end of this book to order those.

Just because you are saved, that doesn't mean you will reach the promised Land. You still need to overcome the wilderness journey.

The Bible says in 1 Corinthians 10:1-5 (KJV) "Moreover, brethren, I would not that ye should be ignorant, how that all our fathers were under the cloud and all passed through the sea; And were all baptized unto Moses in the cloud and in the sea; And did all eat the same spiritual meal; And did all drink the same spiritual drink: for they drank from that spiritual rock that followed them: and that Rock was Christ. But with many of them God was not well-pleased: for they were overthrown in the wilderness."

I believe the majority of the church spends their lives wandering around in the wilderness. In the verses above, the Bible says, God was not pleased with many of them who came out of Egypt. He was pleased to save them out of Egypt, but not out of the wilderness. What caused Him to be displeased? I believe they were caught up by the things they received from Egypt, and didn't pay attention to why God had brought them out of Egypt.

They were short-sighted, and lived only for the satisfaction of their immediate needs. They forgot the great salvation they experienced being delivered from Egypt. They forgot every miracle God had done for them. They murmured and complained and stirred up the anger of God to come upon them. It was not God's will for them to perish in the wilderness. They made that choice for themselves.

God's intention for each of us is to possess the Promised Land. It is not His perfect will for us to perish in the wilderness. The example of how the Israelites came out Egypt is an example of our redemption in Christ.

God has taught us through His Word how we can go through the wilderness victoriously, and reach our destinies.

CHAPTER EIGHT

Seeing and Entering the Kingdom of God

I found out lately, that just going to a church building every Sunday, singing songs, and hearing a twenty-minute sermon won't get me anywhere in my spiritual life. I have to be in the Kingdom of God for me to enjoy the blessings that God has promised me. Coming to church meetings regularly, won't necessarily make a person live in the things of the Kingdom.

Most of the church "thing" that we do today has nothing to do with the church in God's mind. Otherwise, we would experience what he has promised that we would experience in His Church.

All of us desire to enjoy the blessings of the Kingdom. God's kingdom is supposed to be a kingdom of plenty, where there is no lack for anything. Otherwise, it is not the Kingdom of God.

Our God is an unlimited God, and everything He has, is without limits. His wisdom, power, wealth, glory, love, and peace have no limits. This is why the Bible says, who can know the depth and breadth of the love of God? It is unsearchable. His peace passes all human understanding. His riches are without boundaries. His grace towards us is immeasurable. The power that has been made available to us, is also immeasurable.

The Bible says the Kingdom of God is not meat and drink, but righteousness, peace and joy in the Holy Spirit (Romans 14:17).

A person who or a place that is governed by God's Spirit, is in the Kingdom of God. This doesn't mean there is nothing material in the Kingdom of God. Jesus said in Matthew 6:33, that if we seek first the Kingdom of God and His righteousness, all the things we need shall be added to us. Everything we need for life and godliness is available once you are in the Kingdom of God.

When God created Adam, he was sinless and righteous. God prepared a garden for him to live in. Eden was governed by God, as it was an extension of God's kingdom on earth.

Adam lived in the garden, until he sinned against God. There are only a few who really walk into, experience, and enjoy the kingdom of God. Others know in their minds what is available to them, but have no clue of how to get it.

The Bible never says that if you go to church, you are in the Kingdom of God. Jesus didn't come preaching, "Go to church for the Kingdom of God is at hand." I am not saying you don't need go to church. But, for the vast majority, that's all they know when they hear the word *kingdom of God*.

The church functions *under* the Kingdom of God, however the church is *not* the Kingdom of God. Jesus said, "...The kingdom of God does not come with signs to be observed or with visible display" (Luke 17:20b). It is an invisible Kingdom.

The church is a training ground in order to train people to live in the Kingdom. If the church is not training and equipping people to live in the Kingdom of God, there is no use for any such church. You could have a multimillion dollar building and every digital gadget you can imagine, and a thousand members in the choir; those things won't make a church.

In truth, the first century churches didn't have any of the facilities that we have today; however, they did one thing for sure, they trained their people to live in the Kingdom. They didn't have a choir of 200 people or a digital piano to bring in the Holy Spirit, because the Holy Spirit never left the church since the day of Pentecost.

The Holy Spirit doesn't go and come back. Yes, you can grieve Him if you do things that are contrary to His will, and then He stops operating in a church or in a person's life.

In the early church, the church was not the building; it was people, who were filled with the Holy Spirit, and who knew the mind of God. Whenever they came together, He was there to manifest the Kingdom and His gifts. I pray that God's people will rise up to take their places and become the church that Jesus Christ started building.

Dear children of God, let me tell you one of the pivotal secrets of the Kingdom.

If anyone wants to understand the Kingdom of God or to understand the scriptures, God has to open our eyes of understanding.

I am not talking about knowing the stories of the Bible. Most of you reading this book know the stories of the Bible. You could even recite at least thirty scriptures by heart. I am not talking about being in church for twenty or thirty years and knowing most of the ministry techniques and church slogans. I am not talking about knowing in your mind the next point of the sermon before the preacher ever preaches it because you know where he is going.

No, I am talking about knowing and walking and living what the Word says.

Jesus did something to the disciples before His ascension. He breathed on them to receive the Holy Spirit (John 19:22).

Why did Jesus breathe the Holy Spirit upon the disciples? What did they receive when He breathed upon them?

If they had received Holy Spirit, why then did He tell them to tarry in Jerusalem to receive the promise of the Father?

We must interpret the scriptures in the light of other scriptures, not independently as we feel. Some believe that Jesus breathed upon them to be born again. I don't think Jesus was training the disciples for three and a half years without their spirit first being born again. I don't think Peter could have received the revelation in his spirit that Jesus was the Christ and the and the Son of God without his spirit being born again first. An unregenerate spirit can never receive such revelation from the Holy Spirit. So, it must have happened some time prior to this experience.

The second thought I had, was that He breathed upon them so they would receive a little bit of the Spirit, or He was giving them a boost, so they could carry on until the day of Pentecost.

I don't think this could be true either, because that doesn't make any sense because Peter and the others went back to their fishing business after Jesus was crucified (John 21:3).

What they needed to go on until the day of Pentecost was to understand the scriptures: the purpose and plan of God for redemption. They didn't completely understand why Jesus had to die on the cross. They never believed what Jesus told them about his death prior to His crucifixion. Even after the resurrection.

I believe the Spirit they received was the Spirit of wisdom and revelation.

How do I know this? If you read (Luke 24:45), "And He opened their understanding, that they might comprehend the Scriptures." The Bible says if the eyes of our understanding need to be opened then we need to receive the Spirit of wisdom and revelation.

Ephesians 1:17, 18 says, "That the God of our Lord Jesus Christ, the Father of glory, may give to you the Spirit of wisdom and revelation in the knowledge of Him, the eyes of your understanding being enlightened ..."

So, I believe when Jesus breathed upon them the Holy Spirit, they received the spirit of wisdom and revelation, and He opened their understanding to understand the Scriptures.

This needs to happen to all the believers, not just the first century disciples. The reason we have so much confusion, chaos, and differences of opinion in the church today is because people are trying to figure out spiritual things in their natural minds. The Bible says the natural mind is at enmity against God and His Spirit.

So, we have arguments between natural minds and spiritual minds. The Bible says things of the Spirit are foolishness to the natural mind (1 Corinthians 2:14).

How does a person enter the Kingdom of God? Is it by just saying a sinner's prayer? What did Jesus say about it?

In the encounter with Nicodemus, Jesus revealed one of the most powerful truths about how to see and enter the Kingdom of God.

In John 3:3, He said to Nicodemus that a person must be born again to *see* the Kingdom of God. He was not talking about entering or inheriting the kingdom of God, but just seeing it.

However, in verse five, Jesus said you must be born of the water and Spirit in order to *enter* the Kingdom of God. *Seeing* and *entering* are two entirely different things. And, the process to obtain both experiences, is also different from each other.

Jesus is saying that for us to at least to *see* the Kingdom of God we must be *born again*. Many have limited the being born-again experience to a mere confession. They think that if they confess with their mouth Jesus Christ as their savior and Lord, they are born again.

Dear child of God, no woman will ever give birth to a baby if she just confesses with her mouth.

Jesus here, talks about a birthing process. Just like you were naturally born, you need to be spiritually born.

In the natural realm, when a baby is born, that baby has a spirit, mind, and body. When we receive Christ, our spirit is born again. However, our mind and body remain the same, and we feel the influence of the old nature as we used to.

In the natural realm, if you go to see a newborn baby, and the mother of the baby says to you that her baby is born, what would your response be?

Similarly, when the Bible talks about *born again*, it is not just talking about our spirit. Jesus didn't end with the spirit, but he went on to tell about our mind and body.

The Bible says in 1 Peter 1:23, that we are born again not by corruptible seed, but by the incorruptible seed—the Word of God. The Greek word for *seed* in the scripture is *sperma*. In the natural realm, if a woman is to get pregnant, she needs to receive the seed from a man. When the seed is deposited and makes its way into her womb, it will begin to grow. However, she doesn't give birth to her baby the next day.

The salvation of our spirit is a momentary experience, but being born again (a process in which our soul and body are being transformed into a new creation in Christ) is a process. To be born again, first the seed of the Word of God needs to be deposited into our spirit, and then it will begin to grow.

The more the Word grows in us, the less dominant the old nature and the flesh becomes. The more the Word is in us, the more we will be transformed into the image and likeness of the Son of God.

I used to think like many others, that the born-again experience was a momentary experience.

A woman may not go through any pain to conceive a baby. However, to deliver the baby is not that easy. To be born again in our spirit is an easy task, but to be transformed in our mind and our body, letting both come under the guidance of the Holy Spirit; can be a painful experience.

Just like a pregnant woman in a birthing room, sometimes we scream, shout, and lose hope because we don't know exactly why we are going through certain difficult situations.

As it is painful to give birth to a baby, so it is tough to live the life in the spirit by subduing our mind and body. To submit our mind and body to our spirit is not an easy job. I believe we go through pain comparable to a woman in the birthing room before we arrive at a state of maturity in the spirit.

I believe there are three stages to the born-again experience. It is not just what I believe. Jesus Himself said it, in very simple language, but no one pays much attention to it.

Just like the natural birthing process has three stages, our spiritual birthing also has three stages. In the natural realm, once the seed is deposited in a woman, usually conception takes place.

The baby is not formed yet, but the spirit is being born in the womb. That spirit needs to develop a mind and a body before the baby can come out of the womb.

After being conceived for nine months, the birthing takes place. It is not an overnight project. In the spiritual realm, when we invite Christ into our life, first our spirit is born again; as the seed of the Word is being deposited into our hearts.

Jesus is the quickening Spirit (1 Corinthians 15:45). Next, the spirit needs to manifest; it needs to break through the confining shells of our mind and body. As long as our mind and body are not prepared to manifest the life of the spirit, there is no difference between us and an unbeliever other than going to church every Sunday morning and doing all the church "talk."

Galatians 5:21 says that if we don't overcome the works of the flesh, we won't inherit the kingdom of God.

We must be born again to *see* the kingdom of God; while we have to be born of water and Spirit in order to *enter* the kingdom of God; we have to overcome the flesh to *inherit* the Kingdom of God.

When you want to buy a house, you call a realtor[4] to ask for the houses for sale. Then you go and *see* the house you like; you *enter* the house on order to see whether that is the one you are looking for; and if you like that one, you buy it, and inherit it or possess it.

Just because you *saw* the house, doesn't mean you *enter* it; and just because you entered it, doesn't mean you own it.

---

4 Real Estate Agency

WWW.THEKINGDOMNETWORK.ORG

There are three steps to walking in the fullness of God. The first step is to *see* the kingdom of God; the second is to *enter* the kingdom of God; and the third, is to *inherit* the kingdom of God.

We are going to see how each one of these steps are accomplished in the light of the Holy Scriptures.

Seeing the kingdom of God — Transformation of our spirit

We believe that we inherited sin and a sinful nature from Adam through our natural birth, and because he lost everything, we also become losers. God sent another Adam, the Bible calls him the last Adam, Jesus the Son of the Living God.

We are naturally born after the first Adam's likeness, and that is called our natural birth. But for us to see the Kingdom of God we need to be born again in our spirit a second time.

When we believe in Christ and confess our sins, our spirit is born again to live the life God wants us to live. Just like we inherited Adam's nature through our natural birth, we regain our spiritual nature and likeness through spiritual birth in Jesus Christ. Just as one man's disobedience made all sinners, one man's obedience will make all righteous (Romans 5:19).

Just like you and I were in Adam when he disobeyed God, we were in Christ, the last Adam, when He obeyed God. That is why Jesus had to be born as a man—to restore everything to us that we lost. If Jesus can do something, I can do it too. If He has received all the authority in heaven and in earth, I have received it too.

Once you are born again in your spirit, you are entitled to receive everything you lost because of the fall. The Bible says in 2 Corinthians

5:17, that "Therefore, if anyone is in Christ, he is a new creation; old things have passed away; behold all things have become new."

Once we are in Christ, we don't live by what we inherited from Adam, we live by inheriting our new nature from Christ, which is the original nature that we had before the fall.

God has given us both natural eyes to see the immediate surroundings and vision which I call the eyes of the spirit to see the invisible. What you see with your natural eyes and spiritual vision will be two different things. When God gives you a vision, your immediate surrounding will look the exact opposite of what He has promised you.

Now we need to train our heart and mind not to depend on the natural sight for encouragement and hope. If we do so we will be disappointed and left without any motivation. We need to train ourselves to rejoice in the hope of our vision in the spirit. Until our natural sight and spiritual vision become one, we will remain ineffective for the Kingdom of God.

Jesus said in Matthew 6:22, 23 (KJV), "The light of the body is the eye; if therefore thine eye be single, thy whole body shall be full of light but if thine eye be evil, the whole body shall be full of darkness......" He meant that when what we see with our natural eyes and our spiritual eyes are the same, we will not be in darkness.

Many limit themselves to what they can see in the natural realm. They have no clue about the supernatural or spiritual things. The Bible says the spiritual things are more stable and real than the natural things (1 Corinthians 4:18). God has given us natural eyes not to live by, but for us to see so that we won't hit things when we walk. He has given us spiritual eyes to guide us, and we are supposed to live by what we see with our spiritual eyes.

The best way to explain this is to think about how a guide dog leads a blind man. The man has the inner eyes and tells the dog where to take him. The dog has the natural eyes and leads the man where he wants to go. The dog doesn't decide where the man should go. The man decides, even though he doesn't have natural eyes, where the dog should go. In the same way our natural eyes should work only as guided by our inner sight or our spirit. But many are led by their natural eyes and don't reach anywhere in life.

After we pray the sinner's prayer our spirit comes alive, and we can see the kingdom of God. Suddenly we realize how dumb we were before and how bad it was that we didn't get saved earlier. However, we won't have everything that God has promised by the next day.

We will know in the spirit that there is something more than this. We expect things to change, and we feel inside that our lives could be better than what we have. There is hope of a better future being breathed in our spirit. We know healing and blessings are available to us, but do not know how to get these. So many people live with that hope for twenty or thirty years, without realizing what to do next in order to get there.

Many slip away from church after a while, because the things they thought would happen if they came to church haven't happened yet. Poor saints! They lacked understanding of the Word, and there was no one to teach and train them to possess their inheritance.

To be born again means to be born a second time. A newborn child doesn't know anything about the world he or she is coming into. They don't argue with their parents. They don't try to run when Mama tries to change their diaper5. They receive everything, and

---

5 nappy

try to avoid people with whom they are not comfortable be around. They cry to show you that they don't like you.

What does it mean to be spiritually born again?

Unfortunately, many people come to the Kingdom knowing "everything." It takes them a few years of defeat and trials to realize that they'd better get some help. Many think that walking down the aisle of a church and repeating a prayer will get them born again. Jesus didn't tell that to Nicodemus. He didn't lead him in a sinner's prayer to be born again and let him enter the kingdom of God

Jesus said, be born again!! It is a new beginning. You have to let go everything that you learned and experienced prior to this experience. Nicodemus knew too much about the law; he was a teacher, but he couldn't help himself. He was a wise man; that is why He came to Jesus seeking help. Others in his day perished in their ignorance though they knew "everything."

To have a new beginning the number one requirement is to put an end to the old. If you don't put an end to the old, you cannot start a new thing. Many do not put an end to the old; instead they drag the old into the new, and now they can't realize the difference between the two.

The Israelites did that when they came out of Egypt. They couldn't let go the old memories and experiences of Egypt, and they got destroyed in the wilderness. God never starts a new thing until He puts an end to the old. Jesus came to fulfill the law, and on the cross, He said it is finished.

But when the church started many couldn't let go of the Old Testament, and they tried to mingle the law and grace. They had troubles between the Jews and Gentiles because of that.

Even in our churches a lot of good Christians live between the law and grace. They have not come completely under grace. They still hold onto their good works and live in self-righteousness. They live based on what they 'do' rather than 'being' what God made them to be.

Jesus said we cannot pour new wine into old wineskins, nor we can stitch old pieces of cloth onto a new one. Both will be destroyed. Jesus called a little child to him and said that unless we become like one of them we cannot enter the kingdom of God (Matthew 18:2-5).

One of the signs of a newborn baby is that as soon as the baby comes out of the womb, they cry. Next, they cry for milk. To Christians their milk is the Word of God. If you haven't cried when you were touched by the love of God, you have not tasted His love. If you haven't cried to understand the Word of God' you have not changed much.

I am not talking about crying because of the problems or trials you went through, but crying because of the presence of God. Let me tell you that when the love of God has touched your heart. If you don't have a hunger for the Word, you are not born again. It is that simple. One of the signs of a born-again child of God is hunger for the Word.

You may be a committee member, deacon or been a church member for more than half of a century. If the baby doesn't cry for milk when the baby arrives, the doctors feel panic, worrying that something is wrong with the baby. You might have just done lip service when you did the sinner's prayer many years ago. That doesn't make you born again. Peter said, we have to desire the milk, which is the Word of God, as newborn babes (1 Peter 2:2).

If your spirit is born again, this means your spirit can communicate with God as Adam did in the garden. In your spirit you can see the destiny God has prepared for you. But you won't get there until your mind and body come in line with your spirit and the Word of God. You didn't get born again to sing songs or to act "church."

What makes a spirit, is that a spirit is not limited by time or space. If it is limited, it is not a spirit, but it is material substance. Our spirit is the innermost part of our being. It always needs to surpass the soul and body in order to manifest its power. Most of the time, our it's our soul and body that manifests its power.

Most of the time our soul and body limit our spirit. When God created Adam, he was capable of knowing and giving names to every creature that God had made. When he saw that creature the next time around, he knew exactly what name he had called it. He was filled with the glory of God knowing God in an intimate way.

I believe Adam could have traveled to any part of the earth in a second, because how else would he have dominion over all the earth if he stayed only in one place as big as an acre all his life? If a man decides to go to Moon, he can do it. God has created us with unlimited potential, and the only thing that has power to limit us—is us

Entering the Kingdom of God – Transformation of our Soul

Jesus said, to enter the kingdom of God, we need to be born of *water* and *Spirit*. How do we get born of water and Spirit?

Some believe water represents our natural birth. I don't think so, because Jesus is not talking about natural birth. Nicodemus was talking about the natural birth. Water represents the Word of God; the Bible says in 1 Peter 1:23 that we are born again by incorruptible seed, which is the Word of God.

Ephesians 5:26 says, "That He might sanctify and cleanse her with the washing of water by the word."

EIGHT | SEEING AND ENTERING THE KINGDOM OF GOD

How do we get born of the Word of God?

Just like the sinner's prayer got our spirit born again, we need to birth our mind or soul through the Word of God. How do we do this?

Our mind works based on the information that is loaded into our brain cells. This is very limited, because each of us knows very little about anything.

Our culture, parents, school, friends, TV and language are some of the contributing factors to the way we think and act. God gave us His Word, who is a person in a language form, for us to fill our mind with so that we can think and act the way God wants us to. The Word lives as a Person in our body.

The transformation of our soul doesn't happen in one day. It doesn't happen automatically; it is a daily fight, and we need to renew our mind with the Word of God changing the old with the new. The Word is the only force that can renew our mind.

Naturally, our thoughts are opposite of what the Word says. Our natural mind that we inherited from Adam says to hate our enemies and do evil to those who treat us badly. The new mind that we inherited from Christ says to love our enemies and do good to those who persecute and despitefully use us.

It is our decision to choose from which mind we are going to operate. God will not force you, and Holy Spirit will not push you. You need to make the right decision by using your brain.

Once we are in Christ, we need to get rid of all our old ways and nature. This is made possible through crucifying the flesh by the spirit.

Once we crucify something, we need to bury it; otherwise, it is going to stink. Jesus was buried in a tomb after He was crucified. How do we bury our flesh and the old nature after we crucify?

It is done through baptism. Baptism is identifying ourselves with the death, burial, and resurrection of Jesus Christ (Romans 6:1-7).

The first thing God asked man to do was to keep His Word. However, the devil brought contradictory thoughts into Eve's mind, and she was deceived. From the beginning until now God is asking man one thing, to keep His Word. He is not asking impossible things of us as some think. He is not asking you to defeat Satan. That was His job, and He has done it well on the cross.

The moment we let other thoughts enter our mind contrary to God's Word, we are giving the enemy a foothold in our lives. How many of you know that when we come to the family of God, our mind is full of junk that we don't want to be there?

Once we are born again, the real battle is with our old mind. Only the Word of God can keep our mind straight and clean up the junk. God told Joshua to meditate on the law of the Lord day and night in order to have good success wherever he went.

Many are more focused on the devil these days than on the Lord and His Word. David said, "I have set the Lord always before me; because He is at my right hand I shall not be moved" (Psalm 16:8). Psalm 1:2-3 says that he who meditates on the law of God shall be like a tree planted by the riverside, whose leaves shall not wither, but bring forth fruit in season and out of season, and whatsoever he does shall prosper.

Jesus said in John 15:7, that if we abide in Him and His words abide in us, whatsoever we shall ask, He will give to us. The Word is called water because we use water to clean and to quench our thirst. Once we are born again in our spirit, we need use the Word to wash and cleanse our minds in order to live a life that is productive and pleasing to the Lord.

Eight | Seeing and Entering the Kingdom of God

Our minds need to be transformed by the Word. There has to be a radical change in our lives before and after the born-again experience.

The true Word does not divide people, but it will unite people. If we look at the church today, the church has been divided into thousands of fragments all based on wrong interpretations of the word.

Do you think if we let the Holy Spirit interpret the scripture for us that He would tell us contradictory stuff? One big pastor told me that he could not come to the meeting that I was arranging because I don't belong to the same denomination. Another friend of mine told me that his church would cancel the meetings if they knew ahead of time an unbeliever was coming to that meeting.

Dear saints of God, I am not making this stuff up; these are true incidents. These people call themselves born-again and Pentecostal or "Charismatic" people.

We label people according to what they believe. Those who believe in the Pope, we call Catholic, and those who believe in baptism, we call Baptist, and so on. Do you think just because you believe in eating fish that would make you a fish? I don't think so.

When we are transformed by the Word of God, we will begin to see the image and likeness of God in every human being. Jesus saw it when He was doing His public ministry. The Pharisees brought the prostitute to be stoned, but Jesus didn't see her as a prostitute; He saw her as His daughter whom He had made in his own image and likeness.

The Pharisees divided people into different groups, tax collectors, Samaritans, fishermen, etc. Jesus saw them all as the children of the same Father. What kind of world would it be if all Christians began to see the image and likeness of God in each other and others?

I don't think we will enter the Kingdom of God if we don't change our attitudes and get back into the Word.

Many come to the door of the Kingdom and spend their entire lives around it. They see the kingdom but never enter the Kingdom.

The Bible says in John 1:3, that everything that was made was made by the Word of God. Psalm 33:6 says, "By the Word of the Lord the heavens were made ..." Jesus was and is the Word of God, who became flesh and lived among us (John 1:14).

We were made originally by the Word of God, but our lives got corrupted and polluted by sin; and sin brought flesh (the corrupted nature that we inherited because of the fall) and its works into our lives.

We need to repair our lives just like a mechanic repairs an automobile that was damaged by an accident. The mechanic removes every damaged part and puts on the new ones. The car will be the same, but it got renewed by the mechanic. When it comes out of the workshop, it will look new, but it is an old one.

In the same way our lives need to be renewed, because we were damaged badly by the fall of Adam. We were made by the Word, and we need the Word to repair and renew our old life. God gave us the Word in written form so that you and I can come to Him everyday and repair the damaged parts.

This is not a one-day project but an ongoing lifestyle. We are changed from glory to glory and from strength to strength, day by day. Every area of our lives that does not line up with the Word of God, we need to change to become conformed to the Word of God.

We are living in an age where most Christians do not know how to read and get the best out of the Word. Most know the stories and parables of the Bible, but their lives have no relationship with the Word.

Ignorance of the Word is increasing rampantly among the believers. I was talking to a lady one night coming out of a church service, and she said to me, "I bind demons and send them to the pit of hell." I asked her, "Where do you get that information from? Can you show me from the Bible that God is asking us to bind demons and send them to the pit of hell? Did Jesus or the Apostles ever do that? She had a blank face and said, "The preacher on TV does that, so I am doing the same." The people on TV are looking for new gimmicks to get people's attention and what is in their wallets.

Most Christians that I know do not open their Bible more than once a week. They are so busy trying to make money to make a better living, they forget that there is no better life than the life in the Word.

The Word is the key to enter the Kingdom of God. Everything in the kingdom works according to the Word of God. If we are not familiar with the Word, we will not receive much from God.

Jesus said in John 15:7, "If you abide in Me, and My words abide in you, you will ask what you desire, and it shall be done for you." This means your prayers will be answered based on the amount of Word that is in you. If our prayers need to ascend to the heavenlies, they need to be accompanied by the Word of God, which is the heavenly substance.

Blessings which Come Through the Word of God

- We are born again by the Word of God. 1 Peter 1:23
- We are healed by the Word of God. Proverbs 4:23

- We are prospered by the Word of God. Psalms 1:23

- The Word of God made us. John 1:3

- We discern by the Word of God. 2 Timothy 3:16-17

- We are cleansed by the Word of God. Ephesians 5:26

- We are renewed by the Word of God. Romans 12:2

- Our most powerful weapon is the Word of God. Ephesians 6:17

- We know God through His Word. John 1:18

- We receive wealth by the Word of God. 2 Peter 1:3

- We live by the Word of God. Deuteronomy 8:3b

Who is the Word? The Word is neither a book nor a language. It is a Person. John 1:1 says, "In the beginning was the Word, and the Word was with God, and the Word was God."

The Word is a Person, and that Person is our Lord Jesus Christ. The Bible says the Word was God. We must give the same reverence to the Word that we give to God.

The Bible says in Psalm 32:28, "I will instruct you and teach you in the way you should go; I will guide you with My eye." This is how way we know whether we are guided by the Word or not? When a crisis hits our lives, who handles the situation? Is it the Word in us, or our carnal natures?

When we are tempted, who answers the temptation, the Word or our flesh?

Jesus was full of the Word, and He was the Word; when He was tempted of the devil, the Word answered the door, and the devil was defeated!

The kingdom of God operates by the principles of the Word of God. Everything works there according to the Word of God. So, in order to enter the Kingdom, we need to pass the test of the Word of God. Without the Word in you, you shall not be permitted to enter the kingdom.

Once you are born again in the spirit, the real work starts, on your mind. What good is a born-again spirit imprisoned in a darkened and ignorant mind?

Your spirit in itself cannot do anything. Your spirit gives opinions, and unless you make the right decision with your mind, nothing will work out well. Unless we renew our minds with the Word of God, our minds cannot make right decisions. Your mind needs to be trained to obey your spirit. Your unrenewed mind is an enemy of your spirit.

Many have a born-again spirit, but their mind has not been born again yet. When you are born again your entire being needs to be born again. In the natural realm, when someone is born, it is not just their spirit that is born, their mind and body come with the spirit.

Our soul is comprised of our will, emotions, intellect, desires, and memories of past experiences. These areas of our lives need to be transformed into the image and likeness of Jesus Christ.

Know this; the purpose of salvation and the born-again process is not to join a church or denomination, and sing some songs and hear sermons. God has given us another chance to become His sons, just like Adam was His son in the beginning.

To God, being born again means to become like Adam was before the fall or to become like Christ on earth. Being born again is a process to reprogram our minds to act like sons of God.

We live on the basis of the knowledge we have. Wrong knowledge produces wrong results (2 Peter 1:3). If the Christian walk is not doing any good to your life, then you might have received some wrong information when you came to Christ.

If the salvation experience didn't bring any changes to your life, then you are not saved. If the faith you have is not producing the result that you expected, then you have the wrong kind of faith.

We are emotional beings. We are limited to our feelings. We determine how we are going to live each day by how we feel about ourselves that day. Some days we feel great. Other days, we start out feeling unhappy, but end up having a nice day or vice versa. We minister to others to the extent of our own emotional health.

One day we are full of faith and power, and at other times we feel like Elijah under the juniper tree, unable to handle the slightest problem that arises in our lives. If the soul is not healed from all past negative experiences, the anointing that will flow out of our lives will not be pure.

Every sin and hurt that wounded our spirit leaves emotional toxins in our soul, which clog and defile the new man we became in Christ. When we come to Christ, our souls, including our wills, emotions, and consciousness, do not change. We have to cleanse our minds and the depth of our being from all emotional debris that was left over there from past experiences.

We understand God and experience Him based on our emotions. God doesn't change, but we feel like He is changing His mind every minute concerning our lives. The Bible says, "There is no shadow of turning with Him."

Many do not believe that God is always good. If we trace back into their emotional lives, they came to that conclusion from some experiences they had with a person in authority.

This is why we all serve one God. However, each of us experiences Him uniquely. If we don't train our minds to stay focused and disciplined in the Word of God, we will not be effective for His Kingdom. This is why the born-again experience is very important to us.

As someone said, "Our life is where our thoughts are, so be sure to keep your mind where you want it to be." Thomas Moore said, "when the soul is neglected, it doesn't just go away. It appears symptomatically in obsessions, additions, violence, and loss of meaning." If we let our minds go unrestrained, it is like letting a two-year-old live his own way.

The Bible says to train up a child in the way he should go, not in the way he is going. We have to train up our minds in the way these are supposed to function, not in the way they usually function.

Staying in the Word and meditating in the Word does that for us. Before the fall, our minds only knew how to function according to the Word of God. It was not corrupted by sin. Our mind didn't know anything else than to think right all the time.

The Israelites were marvelously saved from Egypt, but they didn't reach the Promised Land. The church has taught lots of people that once they come to church and give their life to the Lord, they are eternally secured. They limit salvation to just a mere confession.

They ignore life in Christ and use Him only as a person who introduces them to the Father. Only two men out of six hundred thousand made it to the Promised Land. Well, you might say, they were under the law, but we are under grace. So, won't God excuse and forgive our faults and get us into heaven anyway?

My answer to that is a big *NO*.

The only difference between the law and grace is that under the law the people couldn't keep the law because of the weakness of their flesh.

Under grace, God is giving us His power freely so that we will be able to do what people in the Old Testament couldn't do. Jesus said, at the end it shall be like the days of Noah; a few shall be saved (Luke 13:23-24).

Grace is not an excuse for weakness. Grace is divine power enabling us to do what God wants us to do. Paul said in Galatians. We should not take freedom in Christ and use it for the advantage of the flesh (Galatians 5:13).

Under grace He gives that power free of charge. You don't have to work in order to earn it or perform anything to receive it. With the Israelites, God worked from the outside to the inside; that means He started from their bodies, and then worked in their souls, and then their spirit. In the New Testament it starts from the inside out. He starts with our spirit and then works out to the soul and body.

The Israelites were made free in their bodies, but their souls were bound by the ways of Egypt. They saw more miracles of God than any of us, but they couldn't submit their souls to God. In Egypt they were controlled by taskmasters. The taskmasters made decisions for them. They didn't know how to make a choice for themselves.

When they came out of Egypt, instead of the Egyptian taskmasters, the system in their minds that was formed in Egypt began to act as taskmasters. They were not in charge of their lives. They were moved to and fro like a ship in the ocean (Psalm 107:26-27). The Bible says their spirit was not steadfast with God (Psalm 78:8).

Many people come to Christ, but they never submit their soul and body to the Lordship of Christ. Their soul is controlled by different taskmasters. Some are controlled by anger, lust, pride, greed, rebellion, their past, etc. I don't believe they will reach or fulfill the destiny God has for their lives. Paul says let us run according to the rules so that we may not run in vain (2 Timothy 2:5).

Jesus said at the end many will come and say, "Lord, have we not prophesied in Your name, cast out demons in Your name and done many wonders in your name? And then I will declare to them, I never knew you: depart from Me, you who practice lawlessness!" (Matthew 7:22-23).

It is possible to cast out demons and heal the sick without knowing Christ! What a terrible mistake that would be! What is the goal of Christian life?

I believe it is to be transformed into the image and likeness of Jesus, the Son of God. The goal of Christian life is not to reach heaven or to have the gifts of the Holy Spirit. Jesus never preached the gospel in that way. The total sum of all His teaching was character change here and now, not when we get to heaven.

Most of the time, we don't understand life in Christ, because we don't understand Old Testament principles. The Old Testament is not history or life stories. It is the exact blueprint of our life in Christ. The flesh and blood stories there are highly symbolic of our spiritual life now. If we understand the Old Testament clearly, we will know how to walk in victory in Christ.

Everyone has faith; even the heathen have faith in their systems. Faith based on wrong knowledge produces wrong results. I grew up in church, but I was one of the most miserable people in the whole world.

I believed everything that others told me to believe, and did everything that I saw everyone else do. After a while I realized it was not just me who was miserable, but everyone who went to church with me was miserable.

They just kept doing what they had been doing; hoping one day everything would be all right. No one dared to question why they were doing what they were doing, because they didn't know any better, and had no other choice.

Many Christians are living a life like the monkey who bit ginger. It was too bitter for the monkey to swallow the ginger, but it was so sweet that he couldn't spit it out. It is absurd; most of us; including me, think that we know everything about our life on this earth.

Others have false humility; they will tell you they don't know anything until you try to teach them something. In reality we don't even know how many teeth we have got, because most of us have never counted them but believed the number our dentist told us.

In the same way when we give our lives to the Lord, we believe what others say about God and the Word instead of getting into it and reading it by ourselves. So, once we are born again, all of our focus should be how we can act like Adam (Jesus) before the fall, not how many songs and worship CDs we can get.

Most believers need to be re-educated from the beginning if we are going to make a difference in this world for Christ.

I was talking to a pastor the other day; he said his church is all about worship. They call it prophetic or warfare worship. He said some people do not go to his church because the worship is an hour long.

I asked, "Dear Pastor, where do we see such things in the New Testament?" There were no worship services as we do them today in the early church. They had more miracles, and people got saved in thousands.

Peter preached at the day of Pentecost, and three thousand souls got saved. He didn't have time to do an hour of singing. I am not against worship; I love worship, but I believe the greatest form of worship you can give to God is through your obedience.

When Abraham went to sacrifice Isaac, he told his servants that he and the lad will go and "worship" and come back (Genesis22:5). He didn't just go and sing "Amazing Grace" or "I Surrender All" without obeying the voice of God.

Today we see fornicators[6], drunkards, covenant-breakers, rebellious, arrogant, and disobedient people who after watching x-rated movies on Saturday nights, run to church on Sunday morning to "worship."

I believe Jesus didn't start the church in order to conduct concerts, symphonies or worship services. We don't see that in the Bible. We don't see in Genesis that God created man to worship Him. Jesus didn't call His disciples to sit around and sing to Him.

When mankind fell from his original position, the main thing that got damaged was our minds. Before the fall our spirit was in charge of our lives, and when it dies, the mind didn't know what to do, so it then took authority over us and tried to control us.

We are in a mess because we are not supposed to be controlled by our minds. Everyone is damaged in their minds until they get to the place where they begin to think like God thinks about us. Just

---

6 sex before marriage

because you did well in school and earned a degree doesn't make you a bright person before God.

Even if you don't have any degree or talents, if you think like God thinks about you, He is pleased with you. Our minds cannot handle what our spirit can handle. When we try to handle spiritual things with our damaged minds, we have confusion, spiritual barrenness, spiritual adultery, and so on, in the church.

This is why, when Jesus began His public ministry, the first thing He announced was to change our mind. It was like He was saying, hey men, what you have been thinking about yourselves is wrong, and the way your mind works is just the opposite of the way I created it. Just stop for a minute, and I will help you change and bring it back to its original position.

Matthew 4:17 says, "... Repent, for the kingdom of God is at hand." The Greek word *repent* is "Metanoia"—meaning to put a complete stop to what you are doing the way you are thinking, where you are going; and forget the past, to start all over again. This means, that there needs to be a night and day difference between the life before and after repentance.

If there is no difference, then we have not repented just "confessed." That means, if you had a fight with your wife or husband; and if you repented of it, you will never go back and mention that again in your life. That is repentance, never turning back to the old.

Imagine if we had a church full of people who have really repented and mean business with God, we could turn the cities upside down as the first century Christians did.

Jesus didn't come preaching about tithes, faith, and prosperity. If you listen to most preachers these days, their subject would be

Eight | Seeing and Entering the Kingdom of God

one of the above. They don't want to know how people live, as long as they receive the tithes and offerings.

What are we preaching dear saints of God? We tell the world to follow our example. Give me a break, what kind of example—robbing people of their money, to pay off buildings and equipment?

How many messages have you heard in the last year about holiness, about being like Christ, about forsaking the earthly in order to receive the heavenly, about loving your neighbor as you love yourself, etc?

How many children ended up in the gutters, taking drugs, and became involved in prostitution because their parents got divorced when they were kids?

How many children grow up in our society emotionally bruised and broken-hearted, deprived of love and acceptance?

These children will eventually become dangerous to the community. Can we do something about this? Can we admit our weakness and ignorance, and ask God for help?

There are no better words to explain our situation than what it says in Revelation 3:14-17 (KJV) "… I know thy works; that thou art neither cold nor hot; I would thou wert cold or hot. So then because thou art lukewarm, and neither cold nor hot, I will spew thee out of my mouth. Because thou sayest, I am rich and increased with goods, and have need of nothing; and knowest not that thou art wretched, and miserable, and poor, and blind, and naked."

Wow!! Dear people of God, the church has become richer materially than in any other centuries, and most churches have more goods than many office store. We can arrange any kind of meeting or program in a matter of time. However, we are wretched; more people are miserable in the church, poor, lacking love and the power of God, and are blind.

We don't even preach the true Gospel; we preach the most watered-down or the earthly humanistic gospel possible; because if we preach the real gospel that Jesus preached, half of the people will not come back the next week.

Naked, but we don't see ourselves naked. We tell the world we are the children of God, and most people won't talk to you and much less listen if you tell them that you are a Christian.

I remember a story that I was told when I was still a kid:

> There was a land that was called the "Land of Pride" and the King's name was King Proud. He was so arrogant that he believed whatever he said was true and paid no attention to anyone's opinion.
>
> One day he called his ministers and said, "I am tired of the style of all the clothes that I am wearing, so I want to announce a fashion competition to the common people and other nations. Whoever brings the best and newest style of apparel for the king will receive a great prize.
>
> The day came for the people to bring their style of clothes to present to the king. Everyone came with the products they had made. The king began to try all the hand-crafted silks and fabricated costumes; after hours of trying and examining material, the king was dissatisfied with all of them.
>
> Finally, he asked if there was anyone remaining who hadn't shown their product. One man came forward and said, "Yes, my lord and king, I have brought you the

most beautiful costume you have ever worn." The king got excited and asked, "What is so special about your product?" The man replied, "Only those who are wise can see this material; fools cannot see it."

The king became very happy and said, "Bring it dear friend; let me put it on." So, the man took the King behind the curtain, removed all his clothes, and acted like he was putting something on the king. After few minutes he said, everything is ready, and now is the time to go around the palace and show everyone your new apparel. The king believed that man because his pride had blinded him from seeing his own nakedness.

The king walked outside to show off the new apparel. Everyone who looked at the king wanted to laugh, but they were afraid of the king. So, they celebrated and applauded the king and his new fashion parade.

He walked through a small street, and a little boy who didn't know anything about the fashion competition began to shout and scream, because He never saw the king in that fashion before.

The king ordered the boy to be brought to him and asked. "Who is this wayward child that dares to mock the king?" The little boy replied and said, "I never saw a naked king before." The king suddenly realized that what the boy said was true. That was the end of his pride.

Why did I share this story here? It makes much sense to me to compare that king to the church today. We are all full of pride and do not want to pause and make any changes. Everyone thinks they are right in what they have been doing and have a reason for doing it the way they do it.

The world has been laughing at the church because we are not able to do what we preach. We are so busy with our own agenda that we aren't paying attention to our own inadequacy.

I had lunch with a pastor recently, who said something that changed my life. He said when he started his church, the Lord told him saying, "If you are willing to give my church back to me, I will bless it." He made the decision that day, and his church exploded in number; within the first three years, they began to build their own building in a very good neighborhood in one of the largest and fastest growing cities in the US.

I had an opportunity to visit his church by divine appointment, and I sensed an unusual presence of God there. The pastor couldn't preach the sermon he had prepared, because the Holy Spirit had a different agenda for that day. Everyone was blessed, and no one complained.

Many pastors stick with their program for fear of offending the people, but they don't mind grieving the Holy Spirit, who should be the administrator of the Church.

Let us run according to the Word of God. Many perish without Christ, because they waited for us to go and tell them about Him; however, we are still in the wilderness, and have nothing to offer to the world.

7 KINDS OF BELIEVERS

Seventh Kind
Saved and Inherited the Promised Land

Out of the six hundred thousand men who started out from Egypt, only two reached the Promised Land. The Bible says we need to be in the group that receives their salvation by faith, not in the group that perishes due to their unbelief (Hebrews 10:30).

God told Joshua in Joshua 1:2, 3, "Moses My servant is dead. Now therefore, arise, go over this Jordan, you and all this people, to the land which I am giving to them the children of Israel. Every place that the sole of your foot will tread upon I have given you, as I said to Moses."

God has prepared such a great salvation for us. Jesus said the way that leads to life is narrow; that only a few choose that way. Great and wide is the way to destruction, and many are traveling in that way (Matthew 7:13-14).

1 Corinthians 9:24 (KJV) says, "Know ye not that they which run in a race run all, but one receives the prize? So run, that ye may obtain." Though all run, only one obtains the prize. In the wilderness race out of six hundred thousand men, only two made it to the promised land.

Unless we reach the Promised Land, our running is in vain. Our Promised Land is the destiny that God has promised us. The Promised Land is not heaven as some think; the Promised Land is a land that is on this earth. It is our spiritual inheritance.

As I said before, we need to overcome the lust of our bodies in order to inherit the kingdom of God. We cannot obtain the promises of God with our might and strength. It is His spirit that leads us into our spiritual inheritance. The wilderness is a place where God trains us to overcome the lust of our flesh.

CHAPTER NINE

Inheriting the Kingdom of God

Transformation of our Body

The third step, is that your body needs to be born again. The solution to the problems that you have in your body, is the Spirit of God. This is why the Bible says in 1 Corinthians 6:19 "Your body is the temple of the Holy Spirit who is in you ..." Not your mind or spirit, but your body is the temple of God's Spirit. The third step to inherit the kingdom is to be born again in your body.

This means to put away all the desires of your carnal body, by submitting your body as a living sacrifice. Unless you do this, you will die merely seeing the Kingdom of God— just like Moses died seeing the Promised Land afar off, from the Mount of Nebo.

Dear saints of God, God wants us not only to see the kingdom, but to enter and inherit the Kingdom. When you are full of God's Word, you will be led by the Spirit.

When you are full of yourself and have five pity parties a day, the Holy Spirit will not even come close to you.

When you are led by the spirit, you will not fulfill the lust of the flesh. When you are not led by the flesh, you will inherit the Kingdom in its fullness.

Jesus said to be born of water and Spirit. He didn't say Spirit and water. He is so much smarter than we are. Through confessing Jesus as our Lord, our spirit is born again. Through renewing our minds with the Word of God, our souls are born again. Through surrendering or yielding our bodies to the Holy Spirit, our bodies are born again.

Once we are born of the Word of God, and abide in the Word, we will be led by the Spirit of God. Romans 8:13 & 14 (KJV) says, "For if ye live after the flesh, ye shall die; but if ye through the Spirit do mortify the deeds of the body, ye shall live. For as many as are led by the Spirit of God, they are the sons of God."

Have you seen people walking around saying, "The Lord told me to do this and the Lord told me to do that"? They will tell you, the Lord told me to wear these clothes today or sleep until late morning. They will add the phrase "the Lord told me" to the end of every sentence. Watch out for those people; it is not the Lord who tells them stuff, their minds have gone off the wall.

One lady called me and said, the Lord had told her to give me a thousand dollars for the ministry in India. I was so excited, and she gave the money to me that afternoon.

The next day, I saw her, and she said that there were angels that came to visit her in her room because she gave me that money. The flowing day I received a phone call, and she told me to tear up that check while she was talking on the phone; because the Lord had told her something different. Do you know what I felt that time? I can't really tell you in this book.

The Holy Spirit is the Spirit of Wisdom and Understanding, and He is the most precious gift the Father has given to us. He is the Spirit of truth and always speaks truth.

He doesn't get into anyone's business. God didn't send Him to tell you to comb your hair and brush your teeth. He gave us our brain to help us to do those things. His job is to help us manifest Jesus in and through our lives.

We need to have the Word in us if the Spirit is going to start working in us. The proportion of the Spirit you have is directly related to how much of the Word you have in you. The Word and Spirit work together, and they are inseparable.

They worked together at creation. The Spirit of God was hovering over the water. Nothing happened until God spoke His Word.

You need to receive the Word before the Spirit comes upon you. The Spirit comes to fulfill the Word you have received. The Spirit comes to quicken the Word, the Word receives life, and manifests the purpose the Word was sent.

The angel the Lord told Mary that she was going to conceive and bear a child, and to call His name *Jesus*. She received the Word and asked the angel how is it possible since she don't know any man. The angel replied, saying, the Spirit of the Lord will come upon you and the Word you receive shall be made flesh (Luke 1:35).

Before the ascension, Jesus told His disciples to wait in Jerusalem for the promise of the Father. They received the Word, and waited fifty days, and the Holy Spirit came upon them on the day of Pentecost. Do you see a pattern here? In each instance the order is the same.

God said in Deuteronomy 6:7, that we are supposed to talk about the Word when we sit in the house, when we walk by the way, when we lie down, and when we rise up. Imagine if we lived with our children in that way, instead of filling their minds with what they see in kid's movies and Disney cartoons.

All born again believers will not inherit the kingdom of God. If it was so, all the people who came out of Egypt would have inherited the Promised Land. Only two did. In the same way, only a few born-again people truly inherit the Kingdom of God. They can see what is available for them, just like the people of Israel saw and tasted the grapes sampled from the Promised Land by the spies.

Our body is a gift from God. It doesn't belong to us. The Bible says in 1 Corinthians 6:19b-20, "... you are not your own. You were bought at a price; therefore glorify God in your body and in your spirit, which are God's."

God is Spirit, and He needs a material body to operate on earth. Earth is governed by natural laws, and it is impossible to dwell on earth without a material body.

Earth is made of material substance, and our body is made from the earth. God made our body so that His Spirit could dwell in us. We are His agents on earth who will do His will on earth as it is in heaven.

Once we surrender our spirit and body, God will start working on our body. In the Old Testament, God dwelt in the temple, which was made by hands. He also dwelt in the praises of His people (Psalms 22:3). He couldn't dwell in people because they were not redeemed by the blood of Jesus.

In the New Testament, He chose our body as His dwelling place, which was His original intent. 1 Corinthians 3:16 says, "Do you not know that you are the temple of God and that the Spirit of God dwells in you?"

We spend most of our time taking care of our bodies because we want to look good before other people. How much time do we really spend presenting ourselves to the Holy Spirit to whom our body belongs?

We forget the purpose for which our body was made. We all desire to have the power of God in our lives. How many realize that He wants to dwell in us, and the only hands and mouth He can use is our hands and mouth to bring healing and comfort to hurting people.

When we use our body for other purposes than the reason for which it was created, our body gets sick and becomes a burden to us, rather than a blessing. Like an automobile if you don't take good care of it, your body will break down fast, and will not run properly. When we use our body only to gratify the lust of the flesh, first it will give you pleasure; but later, it will bring pain (1 Corinthians 6:13b).

God will allow us to go through difficult times until we reach the place to say what David said in Psalm 63:1, "Oh, God, You are my God; early will I seek you; my soul thirsts for you; my flesh longs for you in a dry and thirsty land where there is no water."

When our spirit is born again, the Holy Spirit comes to our spirit, but He will not manifest His power through us. We need to train our mind to think and act according to the Word of God. Then we are ready for God to pour His Spirit upon us.

Jesus said in Acts 1:8, "You shall receive power when the Holy Spirit comes upon you …" We will have the power of God only when the Holy Spirit comes upon us.

There is a difference between the Holy Spirit coming *in* you and *upon* you. He comes in when we surrender our spirit to the Lord, and He comes upon us when we surrender our body to Him.

God's Spirit is a "holy" Spirit and His dwelling place needs to be holy. God's power is available to anyone who needs it. The only requirement is, He needs a body that is totally surrendered to Him.

The Bible says God's eyes run to and fro across the earth to find people whose heart is perfect toward Him, so that He can show Himself great on their behalf.

The world around us is hurting and dying without the love and power of God. The only solution to the chaotic situation of our world is the power of God. We are the only people God can use if He needs to touch someone. What we can do without the power of God is limited.

For us to inherit the kingdom of God, we need the power of God to defeat the enemy who is holding back our inheritance. The Israelites reached the Promised Land, but they needed to drive out the inhabitants before they could possess the land. The inhabitants were too strong and outnumbered them, but they were defeated because of the power of God.

In the same way, when we surrender our body to the Holy spirit, there is no enemy that will be too strong for us to defeat.

There won't be any wall too high for us to jump over. There won't be any challenge that we can't overcome. As the Bible says, all things are possible with God.

When we surrender our lives, it is no longer we who live but God living through us. We exchange our weakness for His strength, and everything He has become ours. The Kingdom of God is an unlimited kingdom.

We can take this world for Christ. God was convinced, and that is why He started the church. He knows that we can do the

Nine | Inheriting the Kingdom of God

impossible through Him, but the question is, do we know what He knows about us?

He didn't start a weak church; He started a triumphant church, and He is coming to receive a triumphant church without spot or blemish.

Are you ready to receive Him? Are you ready for His coming?

It doesn't matter what you have been through and where you are in life. God has chosen you and appointed you to bear fruit for His kingdom. He said we are salt of the earth, and what good is salt without its flavor? The power and love of God give us the flavor that preserves the earth.

God has sanctified us and made us holy. 1 Corinthians 6:11 says, "... But you were washed, but you were sanctified, but you were justified in the name of the Lord Jesus and by the Spirit of our God." So, let us overcome the accuser that accuses us in our hearts, and let us overcome the spirit of condemnation that condemns our hearts.

The Bible says, "Who shall bring a charge against God's elect? It is God who justifies. Who is he that condemns? It is Christ who died, and furthermore is also risen, who is even at the right hand of God, who also makes intercession for us." (Romans 8:33-34).

The Apostle Paul talks about inheriting the kingdom of God in 1 Corinthians 6:9-10.

> Do you not know that the unrighteous will not inherit the kingdom of God? Do not be deceived. Neither fornicators, nor idolaters, nor adulterers, nor homosexuals, nor sodomites, nor thieves, nor covetous, nor drunkards, nor revilers, nor extortioners will inherit the kingdom of God.

Inheriting the kingdom does not mean going to heaven after you die. That is what many people think. Rather, it is talking about something that needs to happen while we are still alive on earth. Once our body is yielded to the Holy Spirit, we are ready to inherit the kingdom of God. Inheriting the kingdom means to receive and walk in the inheritance the Lord has prepared for us now as His sons and daughters.

This happens when we begin to walk in and fulfill the calling the Lord has on our lives. The more we live it out, the more blessings and favor will be added to us. Thus, we will see the fulfillment of what Jesus said in Matthew 6:33. When we seek the kingdom of God and His righteousness, all the things we need, will be added to us.

Once you read this book, whichever level you are in or whatever kind of believer you are, there is hope. You don't need to stay where you are. You can make progress by God's grace. First, we need to know where we are—the awareness. Once we are aware of where we are and what is happening around us, we can make decisions to go to the next level.

We have prepared courses and materials to help you go to the next level. I would strongly encourage you to step into the process and tap into the resources that are made available. To possess everything God has made available to you in Christ Jesus, go to www.Treeof-Life.com to initiate the journey. Thank you.

More Books & Resources

DISCIPLING NATIONS SERIES

Kingdom Mandate (for any donation)
Discovering the Lost Kingdom (Volume 1) $14.00
Purpose, Calling, and Gifts (Volume 2) $15.00
God's Original Design (Volume 3) $20.00
Seeing, Entering, and Manifesting the Kingdom of God (Volume 4) $20.00
The Ekklesia (Volume 5) $30.00
The Gospel of the Kingdom (Volume 6) $20.00
Power and Authority of the Church (Volume 7) $15.00
Kingdom Family (Volume 8) $15.00
The Birthing of a Kingdom Nation (Volume 9) $20.00
What Happened to God? (Volume 10) $20.00
7 Dimensions and Operations of the Kingdom of God (Volume 11) $15.00
Kingdom Economy (Volume 12) $15.00
Kingdom Government (Volume 13) $15.00
Releasing Kings and Queens into God's Original Intent (Volume 14) $10.00
Kingdom Secrets to Restoring Nations Back to God (Volume 15) $20.00
Keys to Fulfilling Your Kingdom Assignment (Volume 16) $20.00

KINGDOM LIVING SERIES

The Three Most Important Decisions of Your Life $15.00
Recognizing God's Timing for Your Life $12.00
Overcoming the Spirit of Poverty $10.00
Seven Kinds of Believers $10.00
7 Dimensions of God's Glory $5.00
7 Dimensions of God's Grace $10.00
7 Kinds of Faith $8.00

HEALING OF THE NATIONS SERIES

Principles of Self Governance $20.00

KINGDOM BOOKS FOR KIDS

Genesis 126 Three Volume Book set for boys $25.00
Genesis 126 Three Volume Book set for boys $25.00

Genesis 126 Coloring Books for Boys $15.00
Genesis 126 Coloring Books for Girls $15.00

GENESIS 126 TEACHER'S MANUAL

Level 1 6-8 years $15.00
Level 2 8-10 years $15.00
Level 3 10-12 years $15.00

TO PLACE AN ORDER:

www.TheKingdomNetwork.org
Phone: 1-800-558-5020
Email: info@TheKingdomNetwork.org

Are you struggling to discover your **PURPOSE ?**
You are not supposed to fit in but stand out !

Sign up today for the FREE Online Kingdom Course

DISCOVERING

THE LOST KINGDOM

In this course you'll DISCOVER:

>> Your true identity and purpose
>> What God is doing on the earth and how you can partner with Him in it
>> Why God created the earth and put us on this planet
>> And much more ...

Why are people becoming more and more disinterested in **church and religion** globally?
Join the course, and discover
what your soul has been searching for all along.

FREE BOOK AND STUDY GUIDE

Other courses available
>> DISCOVERING PURPOSE, CALLING AND GIFTS
>> SEEING, ENTERING AND MANIFESTING THE KINGDOM
>> GOD'S ORIGINAL DESIGN
>> The Ekklesia
>> The Next move of GOD
   And more ...

Register Now @ **www.TheKingdomUniversity.org**

Welcome to
KINGDOM DELIVERANCE
— WORKSHOP —

Are you tired of waiting and looking for breakthroughs? Kingdom of God has the answer.

This kingdom deconstruct workshop is divided into EIGHT major categories which deal with the seven major areas of our life. Each one is connected to the next, and so if one of these areas dysfunctions, it will affect all other areas of your life.

1. Relationship with the Father
2. Spiritual Healing
3. Emotional Healing
4. Purpose and Calling
5. Mastering Gifts and Skills
6. Finances—Learning to Live in Kingdom Economy
7. Healing Relationships
8. Physical Health

Take action now. Order all 8 workshop manuals today !

Thank you so much for taking the courses from The Kingdom University. Taking a course is only the first step. We are pleased to present you with the next step—that of going through the process to get rid of all the extra weights that have been slowing and hindering you from fully living out your kingdom assignment.

Call 1 800 558 5020   www.TheKingdomNetwork.org

www.ingramcontent.com/pod-product-compliance
Lightning Source LLC
Chambersburg PA
CBHW070101080526
44586CB00013B/1143